Gymkhanas and Rally Games

© 1993 The Pony Club
First published 1989
Updated, in paperback format, 1993
Revised 2001

British Library Cataloguing in Publication Data.
A catalogue record for this book is available
from the British Library.

ISBN 0-9537167-4-0

Text by Toni Webber
Designed by Alan Hamp
Line drawings by Sally Bell and Carole Vincer
Photographs by Shona Wood and Maurice Healey
Cover photograph by Richard Cassan

Printed and bound in Great Britain
by Westway Offset Limited

Contents

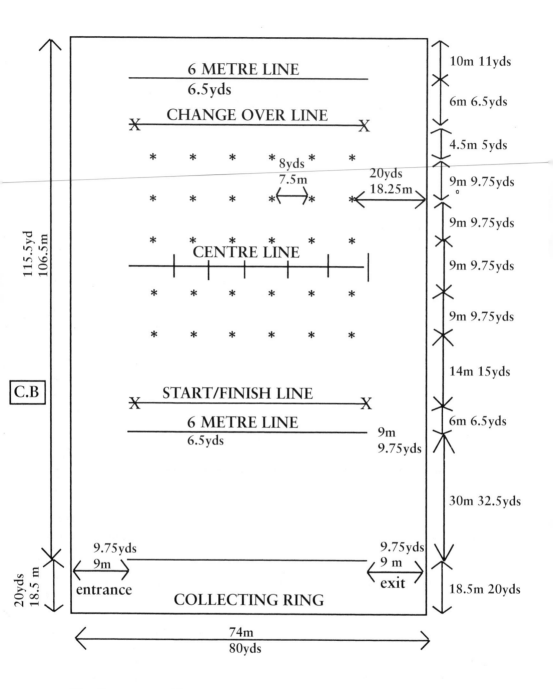

6 METRE LINE
6.5yds

CHANGE OVER LINE

8yds
7.5m

20yds
18.25m

CENTRE LINE

START/FINISH LINE

6 METRE LINE
6.5yds

9m
9.75yds

9.75yds
9m
entrance

9.75yds
9 m
exit

COLLECTING RING

115.5yd
106.5m

C.B

20yds
18.5 m

10m 11yds

6m 6.5yds

4.5m 5yds

9m 9.75yds

9m 9.75yds

9m 9.75yds

9m 9.75yds

14m 15yds

6m 6.5yds

30m 32.5yds

18.5m 20yds

74m
80yds

CB = Commentators' box
✻ = Bending posts
+ = Centre of lane markers for non-bending events
X = Corner marker posts

Plan for Prince Philip Mounted Games arena

Introduction

In 1957 the Duke of Edinburgh presented a cup to the Pony Club for a mounted games competition. Teams of five young riders on ordinary ponies would compete in qualifying rounds and the six best would arrive at the Horse of the Year Show in October to vie for what was to become the most highly prized trophy in gymkhana history.

The essence of the Prince Philip Cup competition was – and still is – to provide an opportunity for the ordinary Pony Club member to take part in an important inter-branch contest on ponies that do not have to be of high quality or value. In 1957, this was of more significance than it is today. At that time, the only competitions open to the average rider were gymkhanas. A few had a go at juvenile jumping in local shows, but the giddy experience of riding a cross-country course, tackling a dressage test, or taking part in a polo match, was beyond the reach of most children.

Transport was a rare luxury. Pony and rider hacked to rallies, gymkhanas and meets, performed or hunted all day and hacked home again. The pony was tough, sturdy and durable, and since no one had any suitable show jumps, no one expected him to be able to jump, except out hunting. The only competition he could cope with quite well was gymkhana games.

In those days, gymkhana events tended to be rather unimaginative. Bending was popular, usually with a line of six poles. The potato race required the rider to drop potatoes into a bucket, but the potatoes themselves were skewered to nails on the tops of the bending poles. The schedule might include musical wands, with musical mats as a variation, but very few races required the rider to dismount and remount, and it was rare to see the high standard of speed and agility which is regularly displayed today.

Perhaps because there was little else for the average pony to compete in, gymkhanas were hugely popular. Entries of forty or more for a single class were not unusual, and the winner of an event such as musical mats, where only one mat was removed in each round, was almost too exhausted at the end to lead the pony from the ring.

The advent of the Prince Philip Cup introduced a whole new range of mounted games. As the Pony Club Committee responsible for administering the competition devised more and more ingenious games, which tested skill and precision as well as speed and agility, the benefit was felt by all who took part in gymkhanas.

At the same time, emphasis was increasingly placed on safety. The general practice of staging events on a circular track gave way to games up and down the arena. Whips and spurs were banned and the wearing of hard hats (to an absolute specification) was made compulsory. Equipment was designed to be as safe as possible.

In the Branches, enthusiasts took over the training of teams. Children learned to vault on to their ponies at speed, the more athletic could pick up fallen equipment without dismounting, and the ability to control and steer a pony with one hand became an essential skill. Today, these skills are displayed wherever gymkhanas are held.

WOODLEY GREEN GYMKHANA
ENTRY FORM

Class	*Rider's Name*	*Pony's Name*	*Entry Fee*

*Total*_____

Name: Rider's date of birth:

Address:

Tel No:

Entries to: Jennifer Smith, Home Farm, Woodley Green.

Closing Date: Wednesday 4 July.

Schedule entry form

Choosing a date for your gymkhana may not be as easy as it sounds. In some parts of the country, you can be reasonably safe in organising an event to take place in the Easter holidays. That is to say, you can be confident that only exceptionally bad weather will cause the show to be cancelled. In downland areas, where the sub-soil is chalk and quick-draining, the ground will not be irretrievably damaged even in a very wet spring. On a heavy soil, however, few farmers will willingly let their land be used for such a potentially damaging event as a gymkhana much earlier in the year than July.

All dates, therefore have their advantages and disadvantages. In early summer, the advent of longer days and warmer weather makes riders eager to take part in competitions.

A midsummer weekend is often a popular choice, but if it is in term-time, boarding-school children may not be able to take part. Also, just because the sport *is* popular your gymkhana could well clash with another, similar, event near by. The end of the summer holidays has a great deal to recommend it – reasonably dry ground, the likelihood of good weather, fewer shows to compete with – but it has one big disadvantage. By this time in the season, many riders have had a surfeit of shows; or, if they haven't, their parents – the payers of entry fees and drivers of horseboxes – have. Your gymkhana may be the very one that they decide to miss.

Helpers

At your first committee meeting you should draw up a list of everyone who might be available to help or who can be approached to act in an official capacity. The following list gives some idea of the helpers and officials involved.

Judges
Collecting-ring stewards
Ring stewards
Arena party
Caterers
Commentator
Car park or gate attendants

In addition, you will have to provide a public address system, first-aid facilities, and toilets. You should also take out public liability insurance, for which Pony Club Branches are automatically covered, and you should let your local police know when and where you are holding the gymkhana. Usually, they will provide a special constable to control the traffic – a great asset if access to your show site is from a main road.

Judges

Judges must be energetic, hard-working and knowledgeable. They must also be fair, especially if their own children are competing in the gymkhana. (The children should be capable of coping on their own, so that their parents are not constantly being pestered by cries for help.) If possible, select a chief judge and provide assistants to him or her. Always make certain that the judges are fully aware of the rules of the games that you have selected; it helps if you can write or type out the rules in full and give each of the judges a copy beforehand.

You must be sufficiently confident of the judge's ability to handle all matters inside the ring without interference. A good judge will ask for extra stewards when it comes to the final. Without mechanical aids such as a camera to record the finish, it is surprisingly difficult to place six riders in order, and it is even more difficult to remember which was which as the finalists mill round waiting for the rosettes to be presented. It is much easier to have six pairs of eyes watching the finishing line, and to assign the responsibility of placing a rider in the correct position to each of six people.

It is not necessary, however, to appoint the six before the show begins, apart from the chief judge and the two assistants. Extra help can always be recruited on the day.

Collecting-ring steward

This is where you need your firmest and most authoritative steward. Experienced gymkhana competitors are past masters at getting into a heat which they know they can win with the least exertion. It is the collecting-ring steward's job to sort the competitors into heats. A good secretary should be able to inform the steward exactly how many entries there are for each class, but if there have been many late entries or the secretary is particularly harassed, there may be discrepancies between the entry sheet and the riders waiting in the collecting ring. Some entrants may not have turned up, others may still be competing in another ring, while a few may have decided to enter at the last minute.

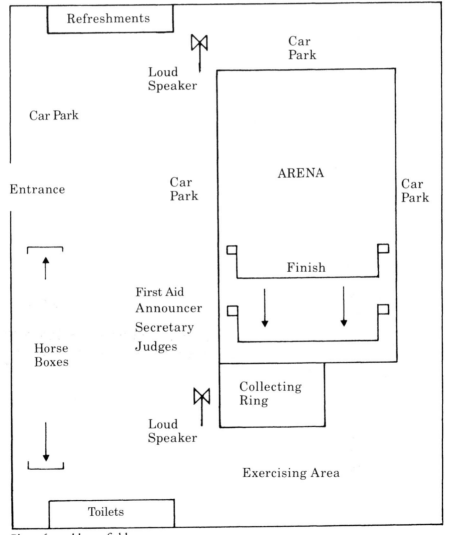

Plan of gymkhana field

The object of the heats is to produce a final of six, so that each finalist will receive a rosette. The number retained from a heat for the final should be the same in each case, and the heats must be organised as fairly as possible. It would be very unfair, for example, to run two heats of six, keeping two for the final, and then find that you had two riders left over who would qualify for the final without taking part in a heat at all. The fourteen entrants in this particular example would be better divided into two heats of five and one of four.

A loud hailer is a valuable aid to the collecting-ring steward, who can use it to hold a roll-call and tell the waiting – and often inattentive – competitors exactly what they will have to do in the race. Even then, there will always be one rider who will ask for an explanation all over again! Collecting-ring stewards need a deep reserve of patience to add to their other virtues.

Ring stewards

Ring stewards are indispensable. They are there to support the other officials, like the judges and the collecting-ring steward. They must be willing to run messages, help the arena party, catch loose ponies, hold ponies and equipment if the rules of a race require them to do so, and carry out these tasks all day without a break if necessary. Most of the tasks are fairly mundane, but they are invaluable to the successful running of a show.

Ring stewards should not be confused with line stewards, who are the arbiters of fair play in team competitions.

Arena party

At a gymkhana, the arena party can make the difference between completing the whole show on time and running disastrously late. Gymkhana equipment, unlike that for a show-jumping competition in which the arena helpers are only called upon if a jump is knocked down, has to be set up anew before every heat.

If possible, the equipment should be carefully organised beforehand, and positioned at the side of the arena, level with the place where it is to be used. If, for example, buckets are to be placed on the centre line and socks or potatoes at the far end, see that the carrier bag containing the socks has been separated from the buckets, and that they are all ready to be laid out.

Brief your arena party carefully. Give them a copy of the rules of each game and let them know if riders have to start a race carrying a piece of equipment. When competitors enter the ring someone can then be ready to hand them the item and to collect it back from them at the end of the heat.

Caterers

In view of current (and changing) regulations it may be advisable to arrange for a mobile caterer to attend your show. They usually give a donation to the show funds at the end of the day: the amount depending on how much money they have managed to take.

Make sure that you provide plenty of lined dustbins for litter – both in the catering area and at other suitable locations.

Commentator

A running commentary is not usually necessary at an ordinary gymkhana, but at a team competition it is essential. At the latter, the commentator is responsible for keeping spectators informed, particularly with the score, and for encouraging the audience to cheer for the teams. You need a commentator who is familiar with the rules of the game, and you should provide him with a full list of the teams taking part, together with the names of the riders and their ponies and the colours that each team will be wearing. At a team competition, heats are usually worked out beforehand, and the commentator can remind teams as they enter the ring which lane has been allotted to them.

Car park and gate attendants

At a small show, these are probably not necessary, since the cars, trailers and lorries arriving are not likely to be numerous enough to cause any problems. If you expect a large number of vehicles it is sensible to provide two or three people on the gate to direct arrivals to parking areas. Most shows allow ringside parking for cars – they have the advantage of reinforcing the rope barrier – but it is better to keep trailers away from the main ring. Your gate attendants should be in position well before the first event is due to start, as many competitors try to arrive early.

If the day is wet and the ground is muddy, the entrance is likely to become quite slippery, so, if possible, arrange with the local farmer to have a tractor with towing chain standing by at the end of the day to pull vehicles out of the mud.

Your gate attendants can also help in an emergency by holding up traffic on the approach road while vehicles make for the exit.

Public-address system

Loudspeaker equipment can usually be hired quite cheaply, both with and without an operator; if without, check that you are being provided with a cassette player as well as a microphone. It is up to you to supply suitable tapes. For musical events such as musical mats or musical wands, the best music is a military march and there are plenty of tapes available featuring regimental bands.

The show secretary is the focal point of a show. The secretary's tent, caravan or trailer is the one place where everyone will come for information and requests or to hand in lost property, so it helps if the microphone is readily at hand.

When the PA system is being set up, be sure to tell the supplier exactly where everything on the field will be situated, so that he can position the speakers to reach, for example, the horsebox park.

Some PA hirers come with their own caravan. If this is the case with your show, it is best to park the caravan close the secretary's quarters.

First Aid

Pony Club instructors and parents should all be encouraged to attend first-aid courses. Who knows when this may save a life!

All shows will need the services of the Red Cross, St. John Ambulance Brigade or paramedics.

A telephone must be available on site, as certain regulations may have to be complied with before a casualty can be taken to hospital. And remember that if the ambulance has to leave the ground, another suitable vehicle must be available as a substitute.

Arrangements should be made for a vet to be on call. At a bigger show there must be a vet and a doctor on the ground, as well as a first-aid tent or centre.

Toilets

At one time, the best – and indeed the only – toilets available were chemical containers in miniature tents. These required careful organisation: to ensure that there were a sufficient number, that the tents were properly erected and would not blow away in a high wind, and that there was enough chemical solution to last the day.

One member of your committee should be in charge of the provision of toilets, to arrange to borrow or hire them, to see that each tent is provided with toilet rolls and, the worst job of all, to empty the containers after the show is over.

Many shows nowadays hire specially fitted caravans, often equipped with running water and flushing toilets. These are a great deal more pleasant and cause less trouble from the show organiser's point of view: but they add to the running expenses, and it is up to your committee to decide the best way of providing this essential amenity.

Tents and caravans

Certain officials have to be under cover. The secretary needs protection from wind and rain for the various papers, rosettes, prizes, etc., in her care; the caterers need a tent; the announcer or commentator may also want a separate home. Tents can be hired and caravans can be borrowed, but if neither is available, an empty horsebox or trailer makes a more than adequate substitute. Remember to park the trailer with the ramp away from the prevailing wind.

Preparation timetable

Show date minus three months   Committee meets to draw up and arrange printing of schedule; book the venue; organise catering, first aid cover, mobile lavatories, etc.; and order rosettes. Send invitations to judges.

Show date minus two months   Advertise locally. Distribute schedules among neighbourhood tack shops and suitable shows. Send schedules to judges and confirm time that they are due at showground. If possible, send schedule out with PC holiday programmes, or hand it out at rallies.

Show date minus one month   Contact all helpers and fix date for erecting arena and other equipment. Encourage older PC members and associates to help with preparation; on the day they may be taking part. Remember that people are often shy of coming forward but will willingly help if asked. It is nearly always the same people who do all the work, so spread your net as widely as possible and invite helpers to bring along a friend.

Show date minus one or two days   Meet helpers at venue to set up arena (evening is usually best). Although one person should be in overall charge, the more hands you can muster the sooner the work will be done.

Show date morning   Ensure that the secretary, an assistant and a gate steward are on the ground at least an hour before the opening competition is due to begin. The first trailer or horsebox to arrive will establish where such vehicles are to park, and you will have little chance of moving early arrivals once they have started to unload.

Show date evening   If you have not already selected and briefed a clearing-up team, remember that you have a loudspeaker at your disposal. Use it before the last event to call for volunteers.

Show date plus one or two days   Add up takings; pay bills; bank money. Write thank-you letters to all judges and other helpers (this task can be shared). Check that gymkhana equipment is in good shape and arrange for repairs to be carried out before stowing it away until the next show.

2
The Arena

A large, flat field with good access is the best venue for a gymkhana, although this is not always possible to achieve. Most fields fall short of the ideal, but as long as you know what is essential you can decide where to make compromises.

The following is a list of points to consider in order of priority.
1 Competition area.
2 Collecting ring.
3 Parking space for horseboxes and trailers.
4 Width of entrance.
5 Access from the approach road.
6 Car parking.
7 Practice area.
8 Availability of water and shade.

The competition area

Always choose the flattest part of the field for your arena. Then inspect the ground carefully for hidden ruts or rabbit holes. Once you are satisfied that the ground is safe, you are ready to make a start.

It is very difficult to judge the size of the competition area when the field is empty. If you start by putting up the outside perimeter, you will almost certainly make the arena too small, and unfortunately this will not be apparent until you set about erecting the equipment. To avoid frustration and extra work, it is best to put up the equipment first.

In Prince Philip competitions, Pony Club rules stipulate that bending poles should be from 24 to 30 feet (7.3 to 9.1 m) apart, with 24 feet (7.3 m) between the lanes. Thirty feet (9.1 m) is, in fact, rather more than most gymkhana organisers allow, but this distance gives scope to a fast, athletic and supple pony to bend between the poles at maximum speed. In an ordinary gymkhana, the space can be reduced to 18 feet (5.5 m) but not less.

Five bending poles are usually considered sufficient, but four may be used if there is not enough room. The most difficult part of putting up poles is to get every lane straight and level with the next lane. The lines tend to converge unless you have someone to help you, and even then you will probably have to make adjustments before you are satisfied.

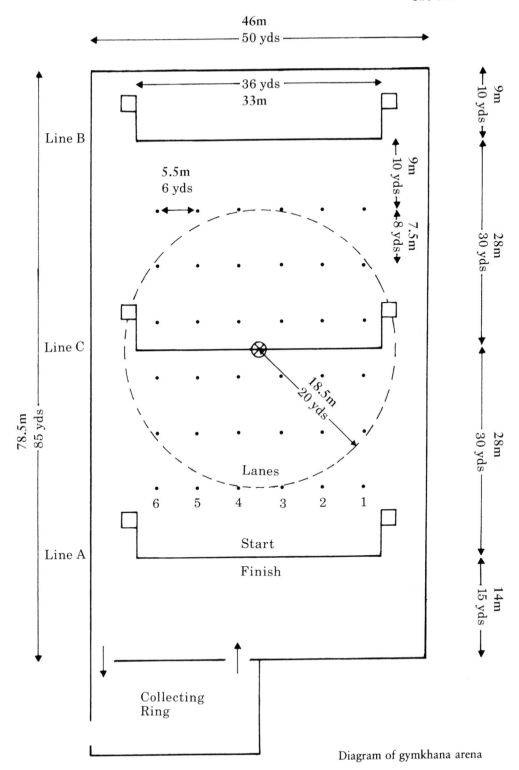

Diagram of gymkhana arena

There is a very simple method of getting the poles accurately into position. It requires some preparation beforehand, but once you have made your measuring kit you can use it time and time again. It works on Pythagoras's theorem of right-angled triangles, and all you require are some baler twine, three metal meat skewers and six curtain rings. You will also need a piece of paper and a calculator.

First of all, calculate the distance between the first poles in Lanes 1 and 6. In a Prince Philip competition, this is 40 yards or 36.5 m (i.e. 24 feet or 7.3 m between each lane). Then measure the length from the first pole of a lane to the last. With 30 feet (9.1 m) between each pole, and five poles, this, too, is 40 yards. You now have two sides of the triangle. For the third side you need to calculate the length of the hypotenuse and to do this you add the squares of the first two sides and take the square root of the answer. In the example, the length is approximately 56 yards and 21 inches.

Your next step is to measure three pieces of baler twine, each representing a side of the triangle. If possible, use a different colour for the hypotenuse.

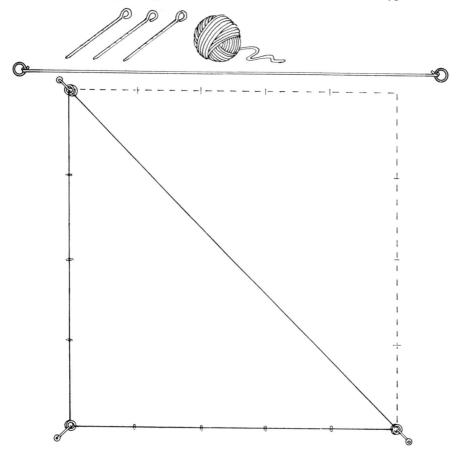

Pythagoras's theorem put to practical use

The easiest way to do this is to stretch the twine along the edge of a table and mark off one yard or metre. Then tie one end of the twine to a curtain ring and count off 40 yards (36.5 m). Cut the twine and attach a second curtain ring. Repeat the process twice more, remembering that the third piece must be the length of the hypotenuse.

Before winding the pieces on to separate pieces of card, you have one more task. This is to mark on the two right-angled sides the exact position of each bending pole. Use different coloured wool or string. The piece which is to be used for one lane of bending poles will require a marker at 10-yard (9.1-m) intervals (i.e. three markers). The other piece, for measuring the lanes, will need four, at 8-yard (7.3-m) intervals.

Your measuring kit is now complete. When you wish to set up the bending poles, place one of the skewers in the ground where the first pole of Lane 1 is to go, and attach the twine with the lane markers to it by slipping the curtain ring over the skewer. Draw the line taut and secure it with the second skewer. Take the second length of baler twine (with the three markers on it), attach one end to the second skewer and walk to the far end of the lane where Pole 5 is to be, drawing the twine taut as you do so. Fix it in the ground with the third skewer.

The next step is the important one. You must now stretch your hypotenuse twine from the first skewer to the third. This will almost certainly mean moving the third skewer until all the lines are taut. What you will have achieved is a right-angled triangle, with the places clearly marked where the first ten poles have to go. All you now have to do is to place the poles in position, using your coloured wool as a guide. The three corner poles will, of course, go where the skewers are.

To complete the other two sides of the square, leave the hypotenuse in position and transfer the second skewer to the opposite corner. Move the lane marker twine to the far end and the second piece of twine to the opposite side, using the skewers to ensure that they are taut. Now you can put up another eight poles.

To fill in the remaining poles, all you need to do is to stretch the lane marker between the poles in Lanes 1 and 6, inserting poles where the coloured wool indicates the right position. Remove all baler twine and the skewers, put them in a safe place, and give yourself a pat on the back for having put up six lanes of bending poles, all accurately positioned, with the minimum of fuss. Best of all, you have been able to do this without anyone having to help you, thus freeing your assistants to get on with other jobs.

Of course, if you plan to have less space between the poles and to make the lanes closer together, the lengths of baler twine must be shorter. Use your calculator to work out the measurements, remembering that in a right-angled triangle the square on the hypotenuse is equal to the sum of the squares on the other two sides.

Once the bending poles are in place, decide where to mark the start/finish line. For Prince Philip competitions, this is a precise distance from the first pole, but in an ordinary gymkhana, you can make it what you like. If the grass is short enough, you can mark out the line with a tennis court marker, or with a paintbrush and watered down emulsion. Use cones or posts to indicate each end of the line. Sawdust is an alternative means of indicating the line but during the course of the games it does tend to get scattered and will need renewing from time to time throughout the day. Any distance between 5 and 10 yards (4.6 and 9.1 m) from the line to the first pole is adequate.

The far line can be level with the last pole or a few yards beyond. Again, in the Prince Philip contests (where it is called the change-over line) this is a precise measurement and you also have to remember the 6-yard (5.5-m) lines at each end. But 6-yard (5.5-m) lines are unnecessary in individual competitions where there are no team members awaiting their turn. At this stage it is a good idea to mark out a centre line, where many races require equipment to be placed. This usually lies about midway between the second and third bending poles.

With the poles and start line in place, you now have some idea of where to put the ropes and stakes marking the perimeter. The rope that you use should be clearly visible – baler twine, for example, is too thin. If you have no rope yourself, see if you can borrow it. Your Pony Club branch may be able to lend you some; you may be able to hire it from your local council; or perhaps you could approach the organisers of a neighbouring show to find out where they obtain theirs.

Wooden stakes should be used, which can be driven into the ground with a club hammer. The boundary rope must be placed at least 5 yards (4.6m) from one side of the lines of bending poles and 10 yards (9.1m) from the other, to give enough room for races which have to be run in between the lines of poles. At the far end, you should allow sufficient space for a pony to run, and at the starting end leave at least 21 yards (20m) pulling-up space.

Collecting ring

A collecting ring – that is, the area in which competitors congregate whilst awaiting their turn to enter the arena – should be roped off. The entrance to the arena from the collecting ring may also be used as the exit, but in this case the collecting ring must be large enough to avoid confusion between ponies entering the ring and those leaving it. Some show organisers prefer to send riders out of the ring via a separate exit, but in either case it should be possible to close off the openings whilst a race is in progress. All you need is an extra loop of rope which can be drawn across from one stake to another. The collecting-ring steward can look after the entrance, but if you do have a separate exit you will need a steward to be in charge of it.

When deciding where to site the collecting ring, bear in mind that it is helpful not to have it too far from the secretary's tent. Any problems which arise during the show can be dealt with more easily if the collecting-ring steward can contact the secretary or official organiser without delay.

Exercise areas

To comply with safety regulations, these should be away from parking areas (cars and horseboxes).

Parking space for horseboxes and trailers

Choose the horsebox park with care, remembering that every box or trailer needs room for ramps to be lowered and ponies to stand while they are not taking part. Drivers will park their vehicles with this in mind. If the field has a number of large trees near the border, and if the ground near the trees is reasonably sound, this is a suitable area. As long as there are no low, overhanging branches the trees will provide shade.

On a wet day, try to position the vehicles on high ground. It is every driver's nightmare to get stuck in the mud at the end of the show, and they will appreciate your forethought if they have a downward slope to give them a start.

The other important point to remember is that loudspeaker announcements should be heard clearly in the horsebox park. It will save everyone a great deal of frustration in the long run.

Width of entrance

Most field entrances are wide enough to take a tractor, and a horsebox should therefore have no difficulty. If necessary, ask the field owner if you may remove the gate from its hinges – unless it is the type that will fold right back against the fence.

Always inspect the ground in and around the gateway. Sometimes it is deeply rutted, and it may be necessary to fill in the ruts with hogging.

Some shows charge an admission fee for cars. If you decide to do this, you will have to funnel the cars towards attendants who are taking the money and issue free parking tickets to helpers and officials. At small shows car parking is generally free.

If you are charging admission for spectators, it will help if cars are directed to a chosen area as soon as they are through the gateway. This can be achieved by means of a short barrier of baler twine and stakes. Your gate stewards should position themselves at the end of the barrier so that cars are not forced to stop in the gateway.

Access from the approach road

Horseboxes and trailers need plenty of room in which to negotiate a sharp bend, and it is easier to get through a gateway on the right-hand side of the road unless the entrance is splayed. If there are likely to be problems, you may have to ask competitors to make their approach from one direction only. This will mean creating a one-way system and sending all competitors a map with the directions and the one-way system clearly marked.

Your one-way system will be convenient if access to the ground is via narrow lanes. Competitors leaving early could have difficulty when confronted by late arrivals. If, therefore, you can arrange for everyone to arrive, say, from the north, whilst those departing head south, you will ensure a smooth flow of traffic. Such an arrangement will require some forethought and a liberal sprinkling of direction signs, but it will be much appreciated. Trailers are not easy to reverse at the best of times.

If the entrance to your ground is from a main road, police co-operation is essential. Lorries and trailers slowing to turn in through a narrow gateway will cause lengthy tailbacks unless the police are present to keep the process orderly. Similarly, at the end of the day it will help to have a controlled exit from the ground. This is particularly important in wet weather when drivers may have to make a run for the exit.

Some County Councils have local bye-laws governing the use of unauthorised signs. You can save confusion on the day if you check with your council as to what rules – if any – apply in your area. Because of increasing vandalism, it is advisable to put up direction signs early on the morning of the show.

Car parking

Depending on the size of your show, you can either allow car drivers to find their own parking spaces or detail helpers to act as car park attendants. At most gymkhanas, ringside parking is encouraged as a row of cars around the perimeter of the ring helps to reinforce the rope barrier.

Practice area

At team competitions it is essential to have space for teams to set up their own practice equipment. So you should designate part of the field for this purpose. If the field is large enough, it is best to encourage practising as close to the horsebox lines as safety requires.

At small gymkhanas, competitors will not need to practise, but they will want room in which to exercise their ponies. If possible, try to discourage competitors from riding among spectators or near to officials' tents or caravans. Aimless galloping around should also be forbidden: it is not only unfair to the ponies but can result in accidents.

Availability of water and shade

Although most people arriving by lorry or trailer bring water with them, a water trough or stand-pipe is very useful. A plan of the showground, with all the amenities clearly marked, should be displayed at or near the secretary's tent. This will prevent endless enquiries as to where the water is.

Shade is important for those riders who have hacked to the ground. If you can reserve an area where ponies can be tied up, try to site it near trees. On a hot day, this may be the only respite from the sun available to the ponies.

3
Gymkhana Events

Nearly all gymkhana games are suitable for individual riders; most are suitable for teams; and a number are appropriate for children on a leading-rein. In almost all cases, the equipment is cheap and easy to produce.

The description of each event lists the equipment required, but for further information, turn to Chapter 6, page 000. There are also instructions for the team version of a game where this is feasible, as well as suggested adaptation for leading-rein participants, with safety very much in mind.

Aunt Sally

Equipment for each lane Two bales of straw set up end to end three yards or 2.7 m beyond the far line • Five empty baked bean tins • Six or more rolled-up socks • Two bales of straw on the far line.

The tins should be placed on the furthest bales of straw, and the socks lined up on the near ones.

Instructions Rider rides to far end, dismounts and throws the socks at the tins until all the tins have been knocked over. Then she remounts and rides to the finish.

Errors Tins do not have to be knocked *off* the bales of straw but must be lying on their sides. The pony must be held by the rein throughout.

Team Game Equipment as above. Rider 1 rides to first set of straw bales, dismounts and uses socks to knock down one tin, then she remounts and returns to start line. Riders 2, 3 and 4 follow in similar fashion, each one knocking down a single tin.

Leading-Rein Not suitable for leading-rein riders.

Ball and Bucket

Equipment for each lane Three or four tennis balls • Bucket. Place balls on ground on far line and bucket on centre line.

Instructions At the signal to start, the rider rides to the far end, dismounts, collects a ball, remounts, and returns to the centre line to drop the ball in the bucket. The action is repeated with each remaining ball in turn. The winner is the first rider across the finishing line, leaving all balls safely in the bucket.

Errors If the ball misses the bucket or the bucket is kicked over, the rider must dismount and replace the ball or set up the bucket and replace all balls. There is no need to remount before doing so.

Team Game Rider 1 starts with a ball, drops ball in bucket on way to far line, dismounts, collects another ball, remounts and returns to hand ball over to Rider 2. Each rider repeats the process, with the exception of Rider 4, who drops the ball in the bucket on the way back.

Leading-Rein Follow instructions as for individuals. Handler, however, should collect the ball from the ground at the far end and hand it to the rider, who carries it to the bucket and throws it in. A ball missing the bucket may be retrieved by the handler, but the rider must always be the one to put it into the bucket.

A good change-over. Handing over a ball efficiently is quite difficult, especially at speed, when the ponies may back away from each other. To keep the distance between them at maximum, hold the ball at arm's length. Each rider must keep her eyes on the ball, or on the hand which has the ball in it.

Ball and Cone

Equipment for each lane Two 18-inch (46-cm) cones, one on the centre line, one on the far line • Two tennis balls, one of which is placed on the centre cone.

Ball and Bucket and *Ball and Cone.* Leaning over as close to the equipment as possible lessens the chance of making a mistake. In these two illustrations the riders have stretched right down without upsetting the ponies' balance.

Instructions   Rider starts with a tennis ball, rides to the far end and places the ball on top of the cone. The ball on the centre cone must be collected on the way back and the winner is the first across the finishing line.

Errors   If the ball falls off the cone or if the cone is knocked over, the rider must replace the equipment, if necessary dismounting in order to do so. A rider must, however, be back in the saddle, with a leg on either side, before crossing the finishing line.

Team Game   Same equipment, but the cones are placed 15 yards (13.7 m) in from the start and change-over lines. Riders 1 and 3 wait, mounted, at the start line, Riders 2 and 4 at the change-over lines. The tennis ball is placed on the cone nearest the far line. Rider 1 has a tennis ball and places it on the nearest cone. She rides to the next cone, collects the ball and continues to the change-over line where she passes the ball to Rider 2, who returns down the course in a similar manner, handing over to Rider 3. Rider 3 hands over to Rider 4. The winning team is the one whose fourth rider crosses the finishing line first, carrying a ball.

Leading-Rein   Not suitable for leading-rein riders.

Ball and Racquet

Equipment for each lane   Three bending poles, 8 to 10 yards (7.3 to 9.1 m) apart, with a container fixed to the top of the centre pole · Four tennis balls,

Balancing the ball on the racquet is not
as difficult as it looks.

Skill in controlling the pony with one   turn round the third bending pole.
hand is particularly important on the

three of which are placed in the container • One tennis racquet with a cross-piece fixed to the middle of the handle and projecting three inches (7.6 cm) on either side.

Instructions Each rider balances a tennis ball on the mesh of the racquet without touching the ball with her hand. No part of her hand may extend beyond the crosspiece, nor may her thumb rest on the crosspiece. The object is to bend up between the bending poles and bend back without dropping the ball.

Errors Should the rider drop the ball at any time, she may either dismount and retrieve the ball or go to the container on the centre pole and take one of the spare balls, resuming the race at the point where the ball was dropped. The ball may be held in the hand whilst the error is being corrected. Should a rider knock the spare balls out of the container during the course of the race, she must dismount and replace them.

Team Game Each member of the team follows the above instructions, handing over the racquet to the next rider. During the handover, the racquet must be held with the hand behind the crosspiece. If all the spare balls have been used, riders must dismount to retrieve a dropped ball. In Prince Philip Cup competitions, Juniors are provided with containers.

Leading-Rein Follow instructions as for individuals. Handler should retrieve ball if it is dropped.

By keeping her hand near the end of the racquet the rider on the grey pony has left enough room for her team-mate to grasp the handle behind the crosspiece.

29

Balloon Bursting

Equipment for each lane On the centre line is a board or sack, to which three or more inflated balloons are attached • A cone stands on the far line • A 4-foot (1.2 m) bamboo cane, with a pin strapped to one end, is placed in this cone, pin end down.

Instructions The rider races to the far line, collects the cane, and uses it to burst the balloons on the way back. All balloons must be burst before the rider rides to the finishing line.

Errors A fallen cone must be replaced. Riders must burst the balloons without dismounting.

Team game Riders 1 and 3 on the start line. Riders 2 and 4 on the change-over line. There are six balloons on the centre line, and no cone. Rider 1 starts with the cane, rides to the centre line, bursts a balloon, and continues to the change-over line where she hands the cane to Rider 2, who rides back to the start, bursting another balloon on the way. Riders 3 and 4 compete in similar fashion. Only four balloons have to be burst; the other two are spares in case one deflates or bursts spontaneously.

Leading Rein Not suitable for leading-rein riders.

The rider must concentrate on the balloon. She should be able to burst it without checking the pony's speed.

Bending

Bending change-over. The rider receiving
the baton (on left) would have been
safer if she had grasped it *higher up*.

Equipment for each lane   Four to six bending poles set in a straight line, 7
to 10 yards (6.4 to 9.1 m) apart. Poles should be of broomhandle thickness
• Do not use bamboo canes, which may splinter if broken and could cause
injury to ponies.

Instructions   The rider bends up the line of bending poles, round the last one
and bends back.

Errors   If a rider misses out a pole, she must return and resume the race at
the point where the pole was missed. A rider is eliminated if a pole is broken.

Team Game   Rider 1, carrying a baton, bends up and down the line of poles
and hands the baton to Rider 2, who does likewise. Riders 3 and 4 continue
in the same way.

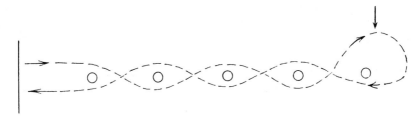

Bending. The rider goes slightly wider to achieve
a straight approach for the return journey.

Leading Rein Very often used for leading-rein classes but has the disadvantage that the rider has nothing to do but stay on. The swiftest handler and a pony amenable to being led will always win unless the rider falls off, which can and does happen when the handler is so eager to get to the finishing line first that he forgets his small charge.

Bottle Race

Equipment for each lane Table or upturned bin on the centre line and another, similar one, on the far line • A plastic lemonade bottle, weighted with sand, to be placed on the nearest bin • An identical bottle should be handed to the rider.

Instructions Carrying the bottle, the rider rides to the furthest bin and places the bottle on it. She then rides back to the finishing line, collecting the bottle from the bin on the centre line on her way.

Errors The bottle must stand upright on the bin. If it falls or is dropped, or if the bin is knocked over, the rider must set the equipment up again correctly.

Team Game Rider 1 places a bottle on the bin on the centre line, then collects the one on the furthest bin and rides back to the start, handing the bottle to Rider 2. Rider 2 puts this bottle on the furthest bin and collects the one on the centre line, giving it to Rider 3. Riders 3 and 4 act in a similar manner to Riders 1 and 2.

Leading-Rein This game may not be suitable for very small children, as the bottle is quite large and difficult for little hands to manipulate. Older beginners should be able to cope, however. Riders should pick up the bottles themselves, but dropped bottles may be retrieved by the handler.

Canter, Trot and Walk

Equipment for each lane Marker cone or bending pole at start and another on the far line.

Instructions The rider rides to the far cone, where she turns, and comes back at the same speed. When she reaches the cone at the start, she moves round it and sets back up the course, this time at a trot. At the far cone she drops back a pace yet again, and walks to the finish.

Errors If the pony breaks from a walk to a trot, or a trot to a canter, the rider must immediately halt and pivot a full circle before continuing.

Team Game Not suitable as a team game.

Leading-Rein Not suitable for beginners because of the speed of the first phase.

Bottle Race. The rider must take great care when placing the bottle on the bin.

Change-over. The incoming rider is on the right.

Chase Me Charlie

Equipment One or two jumps, set up on opposite sides of the arena, with their poles at the lowest height • Extra poles and suitable fillers should be close by, ready for use later.

Instructions Riders proceed in turn round the arena, in follow-my-leader fashion, jumping the jumps as they come to them. When all riders have negotiated both obstacles, the jumps are raised one hole. Thereafter the fences are raised at the end of each round.

Errors Any pony refusing, running out or knocking a jump down is eliminated. The winner is the last combination left in.

Team Game Not suitable as a team game.

Leading-Rein Not suitable for leading-rein riders.

Coloured Corners

Equipment A different coloured balloon or flag at each corner of a rectangle or square • Music, hooter or whistle audible to all competitors • Box or bag containing counters or balls in colours which match the balloons or flags.

Instructions Riders follow one another in single file round the perimeter of the square. When the music stops or the hooter or whistle sounds, each rider makes her way to one of the corners marked by a balloon or flag. A helper takes one of the counters from the bag and announces its colour. All riders standing in the corner of that colour are out. The music resumes and the riders proceed round the square again. The game continues until only one rider is left in.

Errors Not applicable. Organisers should note, however, that this game is suitable principally for leading-rein children, as no skill is required to play it. As the numbers reduce, riders should be asked not to crowd into one corner, but to look around and see if any corner is vacant. The helper in charge of the music should make certain that riders have time to get to a corner before starting the music again.

Team Game Not suitable as a team game.

Leading-Rein See above.

Crossing the River

Equipment   Two jumping poles – the 'river' – laid on the ground about 30 feet (9.1 m) apart • Cones marking a circular arena • Music, hooter or whistle.

Instructions   Riders proceed in single file around the arena. When they reach the 'river' they pass through it as quickly as possible. When the music stops or the hooter or whistle sounds, all riders must halt. Any rider caught in the 'river', even with only one foot, is eliminated. The music resumes and the riders continue around the arena, dropping out if they are in the river when the signal is given. Eventually only one rider – the winner – will be left.

Errors   None likely. NOTE: this is another good game for beginners.

Team Game   Not suitable as a team game.

Leading-Rein   See above.

Riders have dismounted and are dressing-up. (See below.)

Dressing-up Race

Equipment for each lane   Line of four or five bending poles • Upturned bin at far end in line with the last pole • A variety of garments are hung on the bending poles – shirt, pyjama trousers, hat, etc., one to each pole.

Instructions   Rider rides up the line of poles, without bending, collecting the garments on the way. When she reaches the bin, she must stop and put on the clothes, dismounting if necessary. When the rider is fully dressed, she rides to the finish.

35

Errors A dropped garment must be picked up and the rider should remount before proceeding to the next pole.

Team Game This can be adapted as a team game by placing all the garments in the bin (open end up) on the far line. Each rider in turn bends up the line of poles, puts on an article of clothing, and bends back.

Leading-Rein For beginners there should only be one garment which should be easy to put on, such as a hat or scarf. Hang it on the last pole. The rider is led to the pole, handed the garment, and must not set off for the finish until it has been correctly put on.

Eating and Drinking Race

Equipment for each lane Upturned bucket on far line · Plastic beaker one-third full of water · A dry biscuit on the bucket.

Instructions Rider rides to bucket, dismounts, eats the biscuit and drinks the water, in that order, before remounting and riding to the finish.

Errors Stewards should watch to see that, as far as possible, the biscuit is eaten and the water drunk. Should a rider knock over the beaker before drinking the water she is eliminated.

Team Game Not suitable as a team game.

Leading-Rein Follow above instructions. Riders may be helped back on to their ponies by the handlers.

Egg and Racquet

Played as **Ball and Racquet**, but using hard-boiled or china eggs instead of tennis balls.

Egg and Spoon Race

Equipment for each lane Marker cone on far line · Dessert spoon with hard-boiled or china egg on ground at centre line.

Instructions Rider rides around marker cone, returns to centre line, dismounts and, picking up egg and spoon, leads pony to the finish. The rider must not touch the egg with her hand at any time.

Errors If the egg falls off the spoon, the rider must use the spoon to pick it up. The pony must be led by the reins, which need not be taken over the pony's head. Failure to comply with these rules means elimination.

Team Game   Not suitable as a team game.

Leading-Rein   Follow instructions given above. Once dismounted, however, the rider should set off for home *without* the pony, which should be led by the handler at a discreet distance behind.

Fishing Race

Equipment for each lane   Four fish-shaped pieces of wood, plastic or metal, measuring about 15 inches (38 cm) long by 7½ inches (19 cm) wide. Each fish should have a ring in its nose • Litter bin on the centre line to hold the fish • At the far end, a 4-foot (1.2-m) high 'gallows', shaped like a T, with four hooks screwed to the underside of the crosspiece • Piece of dowelling, three feet (90 cm) long, with a small hook at one end.

Instructions   Holding the 'fishing rod', the rider rides to the bin and hooks out a fish, which she then carries on the end of the rod to the 'gallows'. She removes the fish from the rod and hangs it on to one of the hooks, returning to the bin to extract the remaining fish in turn. When all the fish are hanging on the gallows, she rides to the finish. (NOTE: fewer fish may be used if it is felt that this race could take too long to complete.) If the ground is too hard to fix the equipment securely, a steward may hold the gallows.

Errors   When a fish is dropped, it must be retrieved – if necessary by the rider dismounting. The rider may replace the fish on the end of the rod by hand, but should remount before riding to the gallows. If the bin is knocked over, the rider should set it up again and replace any spilled fish before continuing.

Team Game   This race was developed as a team game for teams of four mounted members and one dismounted. The dismounted member holds the gallows. Rider 1 carries the rod, collects a fish from the bin and takes it to the gallows, where the fifth member, holding the gallows, takes the fish from the rod and hangs it on one of the hooks. Rider 1 must wait behind the change-over line until the fish is safely in place before galloping back to the start and handing the rod to Rider 2, who continues in the same way. Riders 3 and 4 follow suit.

Leading-Rein   Not suitable for beginners.

Five Flag Race

See **Flag Race** *(Version 1)* on next page

Flag Race (Version 1)

Also known as 'Five Flag Race'

Equipment for each lane   Two cones cut down so that the top openings are about four inches (10 cm) in diameter. One cone on the centre line, one on the far line · Three flags, on four-foot (1.2-m), canes, two of which are in the cone on the centre line.

Instructions   The rider carries a flag to the far line and places it in the cone. She returns to the centre line, retrieves a flag and transfers it to the far cone. She then gallops to the finish, picking up the third flag on the way.

Errors   All mistakes – fallen cone, dropped flag or picking two flags up at once – must be corrected as soon as they occur. If the cone is tipped over as the rider collects the last flag, she must return and set it upright.

Team Game   When played as a team game, this competition is known as the 'Five Flag Race'. The far cone is placed two yards (1.8 m) beyond the change-over line. Four flags are put in the centre cone. Rider 1 starts with the fifth flag and deposits it in the furthest cone. She collects a flag from the centre cone, rides to the finishing line and hands it to Rider 2 who repeats the process, followed in turn by Riders 3 and 4. When Rider 4 reaches the finish, four flags should be in the far cone, with the fifth in her hand.

Leading-Rein   Follow instructions as for individual competitors. Dropped flags or fallen cones should be replaced by the handlers.

Flag Race. The rider, at speed, keeps her eye firmly on the flag. Having grasped it, she will raise and flick the end back to avoid knocking over the cone.

Speared litter may be pushed off the cane into the bin, using the other hand. At all other times, fallen litter must be picked up with the cane.

Team Game Five pieces of litter (one spare) are placed on the change-over line. One bin (as described above) is placed on the centre line. Rider 1 holds a cane, rides to the far end, collects a piece of litter and deposits it in the bin on the way back, handing the cane to the next rider. Riders 2, 3 and 4 follow suit. When the fourth rider crosses the finishing line, carrying the cane, there should be four pieces of litter in the bin. Errors should be corrected as soon as they occur.

Leading-Rein This is a very difficult game for beginners, mainly because picking up litter with a cane is not easy, even when the pony is being controlled by a handler. Small riders in particular could find it frustrating, and for this reason it is not recommended as a leading-rein competition.

Litter Race (Version 2)

Equipment for each lane Bin on start line • Ten or more pieces of litter (one-litre plastic washing-up liquid bottles, cut off at the shoulder), heaped on the centre line • 4-foot (1.2-m) cane, taped at each end • For the judge: stopwatch, whistle.

Instructions Rider uses cane to collect as much litter as possible and deposits it in bin in a given time, say 1½ or 2 minutes. A whistle blast indicates when time is up, at which point all litter in the bin is counted and recorded. Rider with the greatest amount of litter is the winner.

An excellent pick-up – achieved by using the forward momentum of the pony to hook and hold the litter on the cane.

47

Having succeeded in picking up the litter, make sure that you deposit it carefully into the bin.

Errors Dropped litter must be picked up with the cane and not touched by hand. If the bin is knocked over, it must be set up again immediately. Spilled litter may, in this case, be replaced by hand.

Team Game Litter bins are placed on (a) the start line and (b) change-over lines on alternate lanes. Each heap of litter (20 pieces minimum) is placed 2 yards (1.8 m) on the bin-side of the centre line. Two canes are needed. Riders work in pairs. The first pair in each team pick up as much litter as they can in 1 to 1½ minutes, placing it in the litter bin. The second pair await their turn outside the arena. When the whistle goes, the first pair stop, hand their canes to the second pair and retire while their litter is counted. The second pair then take over and collect litter for the same period of time as the first pair. At the end, the amount of litter collected by both pairs is added together. If a bin is knocked over, the rider concerned dismounts and sets up the bin, replacing any spilled litter by hand. The second rider may not deposit any litter while this is going on. NOTE TO ORGANISERS: this race has a notable disadvantage in that good teams tend to collect the same amount of litter in the time allowed. Points therefore have to be divided, and no team emerges as a clear winner.

Leading-Rein Not suitable for leading-rein riders.

Moat and Castle

Equipment for each lane Cone on far line · Bucket on centre line half full of water on which two tennis balls are floated.

Instructions   Rider rides to bucket, retrieves a tennis ball (dismounting if necessary) and continues to cone, where she places the ball on the top (NOTE: rider must remount before reaching the cone). She then collects the second ball on the way back.

Errors   If the balls falls off the cone or if the cone is knocked over, the rider must replace the equipment immediately. If all the water in the bucket is spilled, the rider is eliminated.

Team Game   Not suitable as a team game.

Leading-Rein   Not suitable for beginners.

Mug Race (Version 1)

Equipment for each lane   Line of four bending poles • Three plastic beaker-shaped mugs, each inverted on bending poles 2, 3 and 4. Pole 1 remains empty.

Instructions   Rider collects each mug in turn and stacks them on the first bending pole. Mugs may be collected in any order. As soon as the stack is complete, rider crosses the finishing line.

Errors   If a mug is dropped, rider must retrieve it immediately and remount before putting it on the first pole. If the stack of mugs falls, the rider may replace them from the ground.

Team Game   Not suitable as a team game.

Leading-Rein   Follow above instructions. Handler may retrieve fallen mugs, but rider must put them on the stack.

Mug Race (Version 2)

Equipment for each lane   Line of four bending poles • Upturned litter-bin 3 yards beyond the far line • Five metal mugs with handles, four of which are placed, inverted, on the litter bin. Fifth mug is given to rider.

Instructions   Rider starts with mug, which she places, inverted, on one of the bending poles. She collects three more mugs in turn from the litter bin and places them on the remaining poles. She then collects the last mug and rides with it to the finish.

Errors   If a mug is dropped, she must pick it up, but need not remount before putting it on a pole. She must, however, remount before returning to the litter bin. If the bin is knocked over, it must be set up and any mugs must be replaced, inverted as before. A bending pole knocked flat or broken means elimination.

Team Game Equipment as above, except that the litter bin is placed three yards (2.8 m) beyond the change-over line. Rider 1 starts with a mug and places it on a pole. She collects a mug from the litter bin and hands it to the next rider. Riders 2, 3 and 4 compete in the same way, with Rider 4 carrying the fifth mug home. Mugs may be placed on the poles in any order.

Leading Rein Follow instructions as for individuals. Handler may pick up fallen equipment.

Mug Race (Version 3)

(Also known as 'Three Mug Race')

Equipment for each lane Line of four bending poles · Three metal mugs with handles, inverted on the first three poles.

Instructions Rider has to move each mug from one pole to the next, starting with the mug on pole 3, which is transferred to pole 4. The mug on pole 2 is moved to pole 3, and the one on pole 1 to pole 2. When these manoeuvres have been completed, she rides to the finish.

Mug Race. The pony is well under control as the rider places the mug on the pole.

Sack Race. Above: A well-trained pony waits patiently while her rider (with rein looped over arm) gets into sack.

Below: With sack well above knees and pony controlled by near rein, the rider heads for home.

NOTE TO ORGANISERS: Rider may start by carrying the sack, ride to the far end, dismount, get into the sack and make for home.

Errors   The rider may not use her pony to get a 'lift': i.e. she may not lean on her pony whilst hopping in the sack. She must hold the sack up over her knees and must still be in the sack when she crosses the finishing line.

Team Game   Riders 1 and 3 remain on the start line, Riders 2 and 4 on the change-over line. Rider 1, carrying a sack, rides to the centre line where she dismounts, gets in the sack and, leading her pony, jumps, hops or shuffles to the change-over line. After crossing the line she hands the sack to Rider 2. Rider 2 follows a similar process to the start line, where Rider 3 takes over. She in turn hands the sack to Rider 4, who finishes on the start line.

Errors   Each rider must get into the sack before crossing the centre line and must have the sack above her knees. She must not get out of the sack until both she and her pony have crossed the change-over or start line.

Leading-Rein   Follow instructions as for individuals. Handlers must wait with the ponies, leaving the riders to run in their sacks to the finish.

Shoe Scramble

Equipment   Two or three bales of straw, scattered in a pile beyond the far line • Six pairs of shoes, a different pair for each lane and easily distinguishable • One shoe from each pair is hidden in the straw • Six stewards to wait on the far line.

Instructions   Rider rides to the far line, dismounts and hands her pony to a waiting steward. In return, she is given a shoe. Leaving her pony with the steward, she runs to the straw and searches for the partner to her shoe. When she finds it, she returns to her pony, gives both shoes to the steward, remounts and rides to the finish.

Errors   Stewards should make certain that riders return a matching pair of shoes to them. They should not assist riders to remount.

Team Game   Not suitable as a team game.

Leading-Rein   Follow instructions as for individuals. The stewards can be dispensed with, as there are handlers to hold the ponies. The shoes should be given to the handlers at the start.

Shopping Race

Equipment   Cones or posts forming a small circle in the centre of the arena. Judges stand in the centre of this circle • On the perimeter of the arena should be nine posts, each bearing a different shop sign – Butcher, Baker, Greengrocer, etc. – and manned by a steward • Cards listing the names of the shops (in a different order on each card) • Pencils, with spares, given to the 'shopkeepers'.

Instructions   Each rider receives a card. At the signal to start, the riders visit the shops in the order listed on their cards, obtaining a signature from the steward (shopkeeper) each time. If a rider arrives at a shop in the wrong order, the shopkeeper should not sign the card but direct the competitor to the right shop. When the card has been completed, the rider returns to the cone or post in the centre and hands her card to the judge for scrutiny. The first to return with a correctly completed card is the winner.

Errors   Not likely. Any bumping and barging should be strictly controlled.

Team Game   Not suitable as a team game.

Leading-Rein   Follow instructions as for individuals.

Shopping Race. The rider has arrived at the wrong shop and is being directed to the correct shop on the list.

Spillers Pole Race

Equipment for each lane   Bending pole on centre line • Eight washing-up liquid bottles. Each bottle should have the bottom cut off so that it measures 6 inches (15.2 cm) from the shoulder. The top should also be cut off leaving a hole 2 inches (5 cm) in diameter. The bottles should be marked with the letters, S P I L L E R S, one letter to each container. Seven of these containers are placed on the ground 3 yards (2.9 m) beyond the change-over line.

Instructions   At the start the rider is given a bottle bearing the letter S. She drops the container over the pole, then continues to the far end where she

61

dismounts, collects the next container, remounts and returns to the pole to place it over the first. The process is repeated until all the containers have been slotted on to the pole and in the right order, the final S making it possible to read the word SPILLERS from top to bottom of the pole. The winner is the first rider to cross the finishing line, with all the letters displayed on the pole in the correct order and the right way up.

Errors   Containers placed in the wrong order must be removed and corrected.

Team Game   Rider 1 starts with the letter S, places it over the pole, collects letter R, puts it in position and fetches letter E which she brings back for Rider 2. Riders 2, 3 and 4 continue the process, each rider placing two containers on the pole.

Leading-Rein   Not suitable for leading-rein riders.

Stepping-Stone Dash

Equipment for each lane   Five or six upturned flowerpots or blocks suitable for use as stepping stones, placed in a straight line at right angles to and across the centre line · The stepping stones should be 2 feet (60 cm) apart · Marker (cone or pole) on far line.

Instructions   Rider rides to stepping stones, dismounts and, leading her pony, runs along the stones. She remounts, rides around the marker and repeats the stepping stone dash on the way back. She must remount before crossing the finishing line.

Errors   If a rider misses a stone, or if she falls off, she must return to the first stone and start again. She must be in the saddle with a leg on each side before reaching the finish, but her feet need not be in the stirrups.

Team Game   Six stepping stones are used. Riders 1 and 3 wait, mounted, at the start line, Riders 2 and 4 at the change-over line. Rider 1 gallops to the stones, dismounts and crosses them, leading her pony. She then remounts and rides to the change-over line where Rider 2 sets off. The remaining two riders follow the same process.

Leading-Rein   Follow instructions as for individuals. Handlers hold ponies.

Sword Race

Equipment for each lane   Cone on far line · Wooden sword, two feet (60 cm) long with a 12-inch (30 cm) hilt 9 inches (23 cm) from the end, inserted, handle up, in the cone · Line of four bending poles · Metal ring, with an internal diameter of four inches (10 cm) and a short stem, attached to the top of each post with a stout rubber band.

Instructions   Rider rides up the line of poles, seizes the sword by the handle and returns down the course, picking up the rings on the way. All four rings should be on the sword when the rider crosses the finishing line.

Errors   The rider may not touch the sword blade with her hand, except if a ring is dropped and she has to dismount to retrieve it. She may then hold the blade while dismounting, but once back in the saddle she must hold the sword by the handle. If the cone is knocked over it must be replaced.

Team Game   Equipment as for individuals but without the cone. Riders 1 and 3 remain at the start, Riders 2 and 4 at the change-over line. Rider 1 carries the sword and rides down the course, picking up one ring as she goes. At the change-over line, she hands the sword, with its ring, to Rider 2 who gallops for the start line, collecting a second ring on the way. Riders 3 and 4 pick up the remaining rings in turn in similar fashion, Rider 4 crossing the finishing line with all four rings on the sword.

Leading-Rein   Follow instructions as for individuals. Handlers may retrieve fallen rings and put them on the sword blade.

Tack Shop Race

(Suitable only as a Team Game)

Equipment for each lane   Bending pole with tray representing a money box on top, 15 yards (13.4 m) from start line • Upturned litter bin bearing a plastic grooming tray a similar distance from change-over line • A second upturned litter bin carrying four items of grooming kit (dandy brush, tail bandage, sponge, tin of saddle soap) 3 yards (2.9 m) beyond change-over line.

Instructions   Rider No. 5 (dismounted) stands behind the far litter bin. Rider 1 carries a wooden coin 4½ inches (11.3 cm) in diameter. She places the coin in the 'money box', rides to litter bin and collects grooming tray. She then takes the tray to Rider 5 who places one of the grooming kit items into the tray which Rider 1 replaces on the litter bin. On the way back to the start line, she collects the 'coin' and passes it to Rider 2. The process is then repeated by Riders 2, 3 and 4 in turn. All four grooming items must be in the tray on the litter bin when the last rider crosses the finishing line, holding the coin.

Errors   Dropped items must be picked up and replaced. Hand-overs must take place behind the start line. Rider 5 may hold the incoming pony when the grooming kit item is being collected.

Leading-Rein   Not suitable for leading-rein riders.

Three Mug Race

See instructions for MUG RACE (VERSION 3).

Triple Flag Race

See instructions for FLAG RACE (VERSION 3).

Trotting Race

Equipment   Marker (cone or pole) on the far line.

Instructions   Rider trots up to and around the marker and trots back.

Errors   If the pony breaks into a canter, even for only one stride, the rider must circle once before continuing.

Team Game   Not suitable as a team game.

Leading-Rein   Not suitable for leading-rein riders.

Two Flag Race

See instructions for FLAG RACE (VERSION 2).

Tyre Race

Equipment for each lane   Light motor-cycle tyre, with an internal diameter of at least 16 inches (40 cm), on far line.

Instructions   Rider gallops to tyre, dismounts, wriggles through it, remounts and gallops back to finish.

Errors   Rider may not run with the tyre round her, and must be astride her pony before crossing the finishing line.

Team Game   Tyre (as described above) on centre line. Riders 1 and 2 wait on the start line with Rider 4 behind them. Rider 3 forms up on the change-over line. The first two riders ride to the tyre, where Rider 1 dismounts, hands her pony to Rider 2, gets through the tyre and remounts. Both riders then ride to the change-over line, where Rider 1 waits while Rider 2 and 3 ride back to the tyre. Rider 2 now dismounts, hands her pony to Rider 3, gets through the tyre and remounts. When these two riders have crossed the

Tyre Race. Most riders are off their ponies, and running, long before they reach the tyre.

Below: This rider has put the tyre over her head and dropped it – which is preferable to standing in it and lifting it upwards.

start line, Rider 2 retires and Rider 3 returns down the course with Rider 4. It is Rider 3's turn to get through the tyre, Rider 4 holding her pony. Finally, Riders 1 and 4 complete the course, Rider 4 dismounting and negotiating the tyre.

Once through the the tyre it is vital to remount without delay. Here the rider is vaulting onto the pony, which has been handed over by her team-mate.
Left: The team-mate has to restrain the other pony until certain that the rider is in full control.

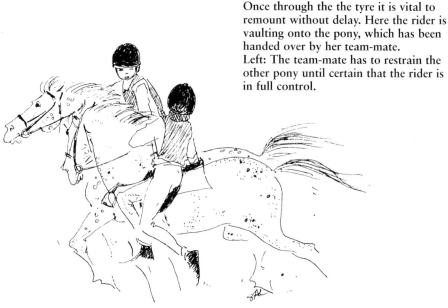

Errors While the rider is getting through the tyre she must not leave her pony until she is sure that her partner is holding the rein. The rein may be taken at any time. Once the rider has moved from behind the start or change-over line into the field of play, she may dismount and run to the tyre. While she is getting through the tyre, she may not advance, and she must be back in the saddle before crossing the finishing line. Both incoming riders must be across the line before the next two set out. If any error occurs, the rider or riders must return to that point before resuming the race.

Leading-Rein Follow instructions as for individuals. Handlers may help riders to dismount and mount.

Unsaddling Race

Equipment for each lane   Marker such as a pole or cone on the far line.

Instructions   Rider gallops to marker, dismounts, runs up stirrups and removes saddle. Then she remounts and rides, bareback, to the finish.

Errors   If a rider fails to run up the stirrups, she must return to saddle and correct the error before continuing. A rider must be astride before crossing the finishing line.

Team Game   Not suitable as a team game.

Leading-Rein   Not suitable for leading-rein riders.

VC Race

Equipment for each lane   Line of four bending poles • Hessian sack, loosely filled with straw and tied at the top, placed on the far line.

Instructions   Rider bends up the line of poles, picks up the sack from the far line and bends back.

Errors   If a rider misses a pole on either the outward or the homeward journey, she must return to the point where the error occurred before resuming the race. A pole knocked out of the ground or broken means elimination. The sack may be picked up without dismounting.

Team Game   Not suitable as a team game.

Leading-Rein   Not suitable for beginners.

Walk and Trot

Equipment for each lane   Marker (cone or pole) on far line.

Instructions   Rider walks to marker and trots back.

Errors   If any pony breaks into a faster pace than the one in which he should be moving, rider and pony must immediately circle. If they fail to do so, they will be sent back to the point where the error occurred or will be placed last.

Team Game   Not suitable as a team game.

Leading-Rein   May be used for leading-rein riders, but as it is not a very interesting race for beginners it is advisable to leave it out of the leading-rein schedule.

Walk, Trot and Canter

Equipment for each lane   Marker (cone or pole) on the far line.

Instructions   Rider walks to marker, trots to the start, then gallops to marker and back to the finish.

Errors   Rider must immediately circle if pony breaks into a faster pace than the one in which he is meant to be moving.

Team Game   Not suitable as a team game.

Leading-Rein   Not suitable for leading-rein riders.

Water Race

Equipment for each lane   Oil drum on far line • Bucket of water on the oil drum • Upturned litter bin on start line • Receptacle, such as a 12-oz (340 g) coffee jar or plastic ice-cream container on the litter bin • Plastic or tin mug • Organisers need stopwatch and whistle.

Instructions   Rider is given 1½ or 2 minutes to transfer water from the bucket to the coffee jar, using the mug. At the end of the time allowed, the whistle is blown and the rider must stop, unless she is in the act of pouring water – in which case she may empty the mug into the jar. The amount of water in the jar is then measured to determine the winner.

Errors   If the coffee jar or litter bin is knocked over, the rider must set them up again. If the bucket falls, the rider is eliminated.

Team Game   Not suitable as a team game.

Leading-Rein   Not suitable for leading-rein riders.

Water Race.

4
The Gymkhana Pony

The most important requisite for the first-class gymkhana pony is that he should enjoy it. If your pony gets as much fun out of mounted games as you do, then everything else is just a matter of training and practice. But no amount of practice will turn a pony who dislikes gymkhanas into one who will qualify for the Prince Philip Cup team.

A good riding pony is obedient: that is to say, he does what you tell him to do and tries his best, even if your instructions are rather confused. If you thump him with your heels, he goes a little faster. If you haul on his mouth, he stops. If you do both at once, he has no idea what you want, but he will have a go at guessing your intentions.

Unfortunately, in the excitement of the games, many riders do forget the rules of riding, and unless your pony is excited, too, he will soon become fed up at your inability to give him clear directions. His movements will become sluggish, his ears will droop and he will be reluctant to leave the other ponies.

If that happens with your pony, you might just as well give up mounted games altogether and go back to the competitions that your pony does enjoy, such as cross-country events or show jumping or dressage.

A pony who loves the games is easy to recognise. You feel him tense up with excitement as you approach the practice ground. When he sees the equipment being set up and the other ponies in the games squad milling around, his head comes up, his ears prick, his whole body quivers. That sort of pony is a joy.

The next important factor to consider is whether the pony is right for you. In other words: does he fit your size and athletic ability? In the Pony Club mounted games competitions there is a rule that no pony of 12.2 h.h. (128cm) or under may be ridden by a child weighing more than 8 stone 5 lbs (53kg or 117 lbs), dressed to ride. Nor may a pony be more than 14.2 h.h. (148cm).

Generally speaking, a bigger pony will be faster in the speed events – such as a bending or sword race – but a smaller pony is at an advantage when the rider has to bend low to drop a potato in a bucket or place a ball on a cone. Small ponies are usually easier to vault on and off, but there is less of them in front of the saddle and if their head carriage is low this can cause problems.

If you are tall, thin and lightweight, you should have no difficulty in riding a pony measuring 12.2 h.h. (128cm) or less, but because there is a lot of you above the saddle, a little pony may have trouble balancing himself satisfactorily, and you will find it hard to make tight turns. At the same time, you will not be able to use the pony for any Pony Club activity other than mounted games: a grave disadvantage these days when most Pony Club ponies have to be good all-rounders.

Small, wiry children, unless they are very athletic, need a pony suited to their size; with a large pony their biggest problem lies in getting on. Even if they only enter events which do not require the rider to dismount and remount, there is no guarantee that the equipment will not be accidentally dropped or knocked over.

So what makes the ideal games pony? The best are probably between 12.2 h.h. (128cm) and 13.2 h.h. (138cm), agile, obedient, fast and brave. They are intelligent, and therefore quick to learn. They are also good-natured, so that they mix well with other ponies and are not put out by being barged or shoved. Surprisingly, perhaps, there are quite a number of these paragons about. Successful Prince Philip teams - particularly those which get to Wembley - have five a piece. They may not look alike - good games ponies come in all colours and shapes - but they have the principal virtues in common.

If you are looking for a suitable games pony, the following guidelines might help:

1 **Size** 12.2 h.h. (128cm) to 13.2 h.h. (138cm) is best, but do not reject a pony who is either smaller or bigger. Some small ponies are sturdily built and very strong. They often make up in agility for what they lack in speed. And the closer to the ground they are, the easier it is for an athletic rider to pick up fallen equipment without dismounting: a great asset when speed in correcting mistakes is vital. Admittedly, little ponies do not have much in front of the saddle, which can make things hard for the rider when getting on and off, but this problem is offset by a good head carriage. Ponies more than 13.2 h.h. (138cm) should also be considered carefully, especially if the rider is tall, even more so if the pony is needed for other Club activities. A supple, well-balanced pony can soon learn to cope with twists and turns and he has the added advantage of speed.

2 **Temperament** Unflappability is immensely important. In team games, a pony must happily accept another pony charging towards him while he waits on the start or change-over line. Mistakes often occur when riders hand pieces of equipment to one another, and a pony which backs off at this vital moment can add to the confusion.

3 **Athleticism** This is not always easy to judge, especially when a pony is being tried out for the first time. But, unless a rider is prepared to spend a long time schooling, the pony should have natural co-ordination and should willingly respond to the aids.

4 **Stopability** Many a promising career in mounted games has foundered on this point. In Prince Philip Cup competitions, ponies must be ridden in a snaffle, although a wide range of martingales and nosebands are permitted. Some ponies have a stubborn streak, and long years of setting their jaws

against insensitive riders have hardened their mouths and thickened their neck muscles. Of course, there are very experienced games ponies who know perfectly well when to stop, but unless their riders have complete confidence in them – something which can take time to build up – and unless they learn how to handle them, they are not much use for other Pony Club activities.

5 Age   No pony under four years of age is permitted in a Pony Club mounted games competition, and most shows and gymkhanas have a similar rule. In general, it is probably more sensible to look for a pony who is at least eight years old. At the other end of the age range, old ponies may no longer have sufficient speed and suppleness to cope with very high-powered competitions. But experience counts, and many ponies have been well into their twenties before retiring from the games.

6 Fitness   General grass-fed lack of fitness is not necessarily a problem. A careful programme of feeding and exercise will build up muscle and bring a pony back to tip-top condition. But beware of defects, such as suspect wind, broken and brittle hooves, puffy legs and – that scourge of native ponies – sweet itch. Broken wind is incurable; the others may be cured or controlled but only at great trouble and/or expense.

7 Willingness   A forward-going pony is essential. Gymkhana regulations forbid the use of whips or spurs. Any rider using pieces of equipment such as batons or canes to enforce the leg aids will immediately be disqualified. Even a slap with the palm of the hand is forbidden. So a good gymkhana pony must have the urge to go fast, allowing the rider to concentrate on the requirements of the race. Willingness also covers such virtues as being easy to catch, easy to box, easy to shoe. Most gymkhana ponies are of native stock and are happiest and healthiest living out. If a pony will not be caught when he is most needed, all his other virtues are useless. Similarly, a pony who is unwilling to enter a trailer or box without a great deal of persuasion is wearing on the nerves just at the moment when his rider is supposed to be calm and collected.

Assuming that a pony answers most requirements, the next stage is training and preparation.

5
Training for Pony and Rider

You have found your pony. He is the right size for you. He is easy to catch and box and he enjoys mounted games. In fact, he is positively enthusiastic.

Thereafter, it is a matter of practice. Your first problem may lie in training yourself to keep up with him. He will soon learn to watch the starter's flag, to bend along a row of bending poles, taking the shortest possible line, and to slide to a juddering stop when you reach a bucket or cone. When you dismount to pick up a sock, he will know that you have to get back as quickly as possible, and as soon as you straighten up he will be off. The only trouble with this model of perfection is that he forgets that you, too, have a part to play.

There is no point in his hugging the bending poles if he does not leave you enough room for your knees, or in galloping back to the bucket when you have collected a sock if you have not had time to get into the saddle.

This is where practice and training come in. Practice is something you can do on your own. Training is what you do with other members of a team. For anyone who is really anxious to do well at gymkhanas, therefore, the best way of setting about it is to join your local Pony Club branch's Prince Philip squad. At any gymkhana it is noticeable that the finalists in all the races are almost without exception those who train regularly for Pony Club mounted games.

One of the main advantages in joining a training squad is being able to use the trainer's equipment. Although you can, of course, acquire or make some of your own, most trainers have spent a number of years building up their collection, and whenever a new game is introduced they add a bit more.

Another advantage in being a member of a squad is that it gives you a yardstick by which to measure your progress. You will also learn a great deal – such as the most efficient way of placing a ball on a cone, or carrying a flag, or vaulting on. Best of all is the sense of belonging to a group of friends who want you to do well.

Team members quickly realise that there is no point in blaming someone if she makes a mistake: nobody does so on purpose. Team members are there to encourage, comfort and praise. They act together. This becomes obvious when a team has to split up because a member leaves the area or grows beyond the age limit. It may take a few weeks for the replacement to settle down and really to feel part of a single unit.

In the meantime, you can do plenty of practising on your own, needing neither equipment nor a companion. Starting, stopping, dismounting, vaulting, neck-reining, can all be practised when you are out on a ride or have half an hour to spare between school and homework.

1 Starting   At the start of a race, you want your pony to stand perfectly still and to move straight into a gallop as soon as your heels touch his flanks. This is not something that you would normally do in a schooling arena. Your pony has to unlearn everything he has been taught before: or he must at least learn that what he has to do in a dressage arena is not what is required from him in mounted games. Take the lessons gradually, first by making him stand while you count to ten, then urging him into a trot. When he is doing this correctly, press him into a canter. Always praise him when he does well.

2 Stopping   In most schooling exercises, the descent through the paces is a gradual process – from canter to trot to walk to stop. Your pony has to learn to slide to a halt from a gallop. You should give aids correctly but vigorously, your legs urging him on to the bit, your hands refusing to yield. As soon as he stops, relax your hands and give him plenty of praise. During these practices, never forget to use your voice – ponies very soon learn to respond to spoken commands.

3 Dismounting   This is part of *your* training, rather than that of the pony. There are plenty of occasions when precious seconds can be saved by the rider being able to dismount while the pony is moving quickly. In effect, you dismount in the usual way – right hand on the pommel, left hand on the pony's neck, feet out of the stirrups and right leg swinging over the back of the saddle in one easy movement. The important difference is that you must land facing forward – and as soon as your feet touch the ground you start running. If you do not start running, you will fall flat on your face. With practice, and provided that your pony leads well, you will soon perform the movement with barely a hesitation.

Ponies with a high head carriage make dismounting at speed a great deal easier. If your pony tends to lower his head as he slides to a stop, you will find it more difficult to land facing forward. With practice, however, this disadvantage can largely be overcome by shifting your left hand from the pony's neck to the pommel of the saddle and placing your right hand just behind it.

4 Vaulting   An eager pony, on his toes and anxious to be off, is very difficult to mount in the conventional way. With one foot in the stirrup and the other on the ground, you can be hopping around for a long time before finally swinging yourself into the saddle. By then, it will be too late. The quickest way to get on, therefore, is by means of the vault. If you are a tall lightweight with long legs and a small pony you may be able to swing your right leg over the saddle and spring into place as quickly as dismounting: but only a few very athletic riders can manage this with confidence. The vault, however, is within the capabilities of most gymkhana competitors: though, like any action which relies on split-second timing to succeed, it requires regular practice.

In essence you are using the pony's forward momentum to carry you into the saddle, but you must see that you are in the right position at the right time. Your pony should be travelling at a trot and moving straight, with you running beside him just behind his shoulder. Place your right arm across the saddle and grasp the front flap of the saddle on the far side. Your left arm is across your body, your left hand is holding the reins and lightly resting on the pony's neck just in front of the pommel. Watch your pony's front legs. As his near-side foreleg touches the ground, jump with both feet together and spring upwards, swinging your right leg across the saddle as you do so. Your right hand on the far side supports your weight and guides your movement as you rise through the air. On paper, this looks very difficult, because each movement has been described as it happens. In practice, the vault happens so quickly that the actions blur.

Practise the vault whenever you can and, if possible, from both sides. There are plenty of occasions when the ability to get on from the 'wrong' side will make all the difference between winning and losing a race.

5 Neck-reining   Almost all mounted games require the rider to hold a piece of equipment in one hand while managing the pony with the other. If you can teach your pony to respond to the pressure of the rein on his neck, you will be able to steer him simply by turning the hand holding the reins from one side to the other. The pressure encourages him to move away from the rein that is resting against his neck. At first you will have to reinforce the command by feeling the opposite rein, using both hands, but gradually you will be able to relax the bit rein and concentrate on the neck. For the action to be effective, you will have to hold your hand higher than usual, very much in the manner of a Western cowboy.

Remember that when neck-reining the movement of the hand must be very slight. If it is too sharp or jerky, you will give an opposite signal to your pony. Hold the palm of the hand downwards and keep your wrist slightly flexed and supple. When you want your pony to change direction, apply the leg aids *first*, then indicate your wishes with a *small* turn of the wrist in the direction that you wish to go.

Team Training

All team trainers have their own methods of training, and it would be impertinent to suggest that there are wrong and right ways of tackling the task. Nevertheless, most trainers would agree that the change-over – that is, one member of the team handing a piece of equipment to another – is a manoeuvre fraught with difficulties. Under the rules of the Prince Philip Cup, all change-overs must take place behind the line. Problems arise when the waiting pony either runs backwards or dodges away from the incoming pony, thus making

Baton changing: correct and incorrect.

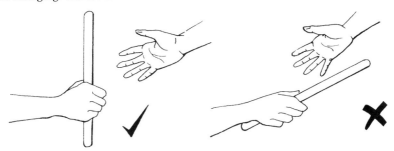

the two riders fumble the hand-over. There is more than one solution, depending on the pony. For the backward-running type, the simplest solution is to hold him well back behind the change-over line and start moving forward as the incoming pony approaches the line. It is difficult for him to change direction at the point of the hand-over if his rider's legs are driving him firmly onwards. Once the hand-over is completed the incoming pony moves sharply away and the outgoing one is already well into his stride.

A pony who dodges to the side sometimes gains confidence if he is placed at an angle to the line. At practice, it can help to have another pony of more stolid temperament standing in such a position that the sideways movement is obstructed. In a competition, however, this third pony would not be permitted.

With most ponies, constant repetition will overcome most problems. If this fails but if the pony is in every other way an asset to the team, the only solution is to place him first in the running order.

Riders can help in change-overs by holding the items of equipment correctly, usually upright and at one end, to give the next rider a chance to grasp it firmly. The flag, for example, should not be held like a lance (a common fault with newcomers to team games). The bottle is best gripped at the top, the baton at the bottom. The arm should always be at full stretch: particularly when the item to be exchanged is something small like a ball, a sock or a potato.

If nothing is to be handed from one rider to another, both riders should watch the ground carefully, as the incoming pony must have all four feet across the line before the next rider sets off. When three ponies are involved in a change-over – such as in the Groom's Stakes or the Rope Race – every part of the switch must happen behind the line before the race continues.

If possible, practise hand-overs so that the rider receiving an item of equipment is able to hold it in the same way as she will do so when carrying out the next part of the race. She should not have to adjust her grip at all. The Flag Race is the perfect example. In taking a flag from a cone, the natural way is to grasp it with the palm of the hand facing forward and to snatch it upwards, flicking the end of it back to avoid knocking the cone over. When a rider does this, she ends up with her hand about 12 inches (30 cm) from the top of the cane, and the flag uppermost. The next rider taking the cane will find that her grip is wrong for planting the flag in the cone, since the easiest way to perform this action accurately is to hold the cane like a sword. If she has to adjust her grip in mid-gallop she runs the risk of dropping the flag. The simple solution is for the first rider to turn her hand over as she approaches Rider 2, reversing the cane. When the second rider takes the cane, her hand will be positioned exactly right for placing the flag correctly.

In all races where an item has to be put in or on another piece of equipment, the *approach* is important. It is best to approach at an angle, steadying the pony with one hand and bending low to get as close as possible to the cone,

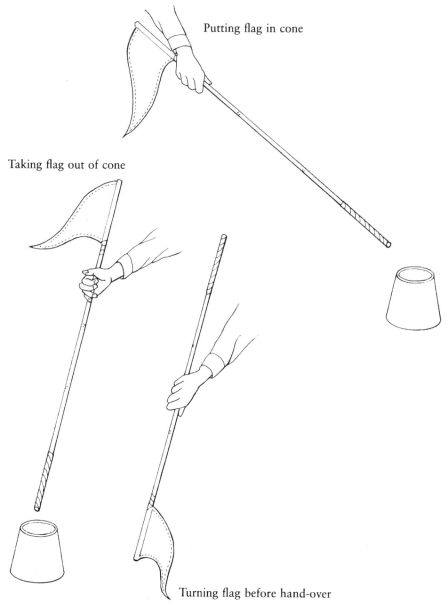

Putting flag in cone

Taking flag out of cone

Turning flag before hand-over

bin or bucket. Your legs must always control the pony's quarters, keeping them away from the equipment. Even the flick of a tail can knock over a bucket or dislodge a ball.

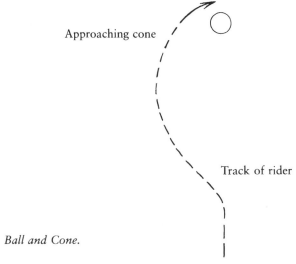

Approaching cone

Track of rider

Ball and Cone.

The games chosen for the Area level of the Prince Philip Cup competition are announced and demonstrated either at Regional Study Days around the country or at a main Mounted Games Study Day at Stoneleigh. Soon after Christmas, the current year's rule book is published. It contains the rules for the six games, plus warm-up race – if there is one – and tie-breaker, which will be used at the Area competitions, plus the ten games and tie-breaker scheduled for the Zone Finals.

At this stage, most trainers begin preliminary training sessions, practising the Area games. Area Competitions are held during April and May, and training moves towards its peak in the last week before the event. Zone Finals take place in August. Usually, twelve teams compete for one of the six coveted places at the Horse of the Year Show in October. It is at the Zone Final that spectators can really spot the quality which separates one or two teams from the rest.

Zone Finals are won or lost on rapid change-overs and the speed of the ponies – but above all on the ability of the riders to make their ponies stop and start at will. If you train your pony to stop at the moment when he is given the order, and to stand without moving until he is instructed to move off, you will have the edge on your rivals. It is easier to deposit or to pick up an item of equipment without mistakes from the back of a stationary pony than from one which jumps around in excitement or overshoots. Trainers who concentrate on *pony handling* stand a greater chance of success than those who merely practise the designated games. Riders can help by practising on their own.

6
Equipment

Whether you are a gymkhana organiser or just a rider hoping to improve your performance, you will need to build up a collection of equipment. Most races call for items which are comparatively cheap to buy or to make, and most are used in different ways for more than one game. Organisers will need a quantity of items – enough for six lanes at a minimum – but the wise will make certain that they have plenty of spares. The following is a useful checklist of equipment:

☐ Bending poles   ☐ Mugs
☐ Road traffic cones   ☐ Balls
☐ Buckets   ☐ Bottles
☐ Flags and canes   ☐ Litter
☐ Bins   ☐ Rings
☐ Old socks   ☐ Extra equipment

1 Bending poles For safety's safe, *never* use bamboo canes for this purpose. Bamboo canes are too thin, too whippy, and can splinter dangerously if they break. The best bending poles are broom handles, which can be painted in bright colours to give added visibility. Poles can also be cut from lengths of softwood: 1 in by 1 in or 2.5 cm by 2.5 cm (1½ in by 1½ in or 3 cm by 3 cm if more substantial poles are required). Softwood is cheaper to buy than broom handles but needs more preparation. The base of each of the poles can be sharpened to a point so that they can be banged into the ground, but for practice purposes a weighted base may be used. In schooling arenas with all-weather surfaces, it is not a good idea to knock poles into the ground, and a weighted base is essential. This can be made by setting one end of the pole in concrete in a 750 g instant coffee powder tin. However, in a high wind or on uneven ground the pole, though weighted, will not be very stable.

Signam, the company which makes gymkhana equipment and whose products are endorsed by the Pony Club, fit metal spikes to the ends of their bending poles, which are very efficient. Signam also make special circular metal bases into which spikes can be fitted, for use in indoor schools. These can be adapted to produce bending poles of reasonable stability. The address of the company is given at the end of this book and you can write for a catalogue and price list.

For practising and to save time in setting up, support poles by placing them in full-length cones.

2 Road traffic cones Cones are widely available, sometimes at builders' merchants, certainly in stores specialising in road repair equipment. Organisers will need at least a dozen for cutting down to a size suitable for flag containers, and a further dozen for races which require full size cones; the latter will need trimming, as the tops are usually closed. Flag-race cones should be cut in half to give a top hole measuring 4 inches (10 cm) in diameter. To determine where to cut the cone so that the hole is just the right size, take a strip of paper or thin card 12½ inches (32 cm) long and paste the ends together to form a collar. Slip the collar over the cone and draw a line on the cone's surface along the bottom edge. Remove the collar and cut round the line with a Stanley knife. Do not throw away the top half of each cone as it can be used, inverted, in the Knickerbocker Glory Race. Cones are very useful items for gymkhana games as they are easy to store and handle and can be used to mark out the perimeter of a circle (for races such as Musical Mats) and to denote the start and finish line.

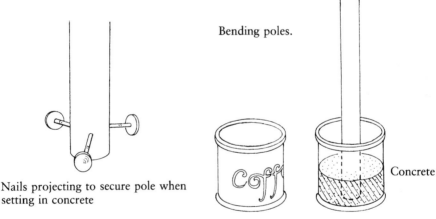

Bending poles.

Nails projecting to secure pole when setting in concrete

Concrete

Road traffic cones.

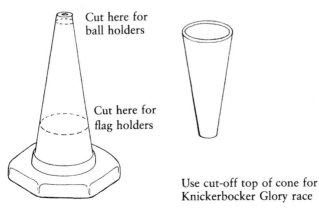

Cut here for ball holders

Cut here for flag holders

Use cut-off top of cone for Knickerbocker Glory race

Equipment

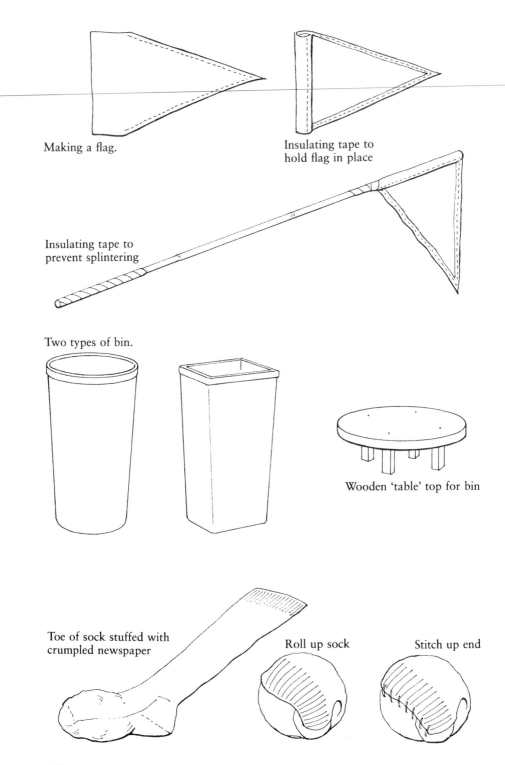

Making a flag.

Insulating tape to
hold flag in place

Insulating tape to
prevent splintering

Two types of bin.

Wooden 'table' top for bin

Toe of sock stuffed with
crumpled newspaper

Roll up sock

Stitch up end

80

When buying cones, ask for the smaller of the two sizes generally available (about 18 inches to 2 feet or 46 to 60 cm high). The very large size, commonly seen on motorways, is not suitable for mounted games.

3 Buckets Any standard feed bucket can be used. Those made of robust plastic are inexpensive and usually on sale in tack shops, but organisers should make sure that they are identical in size and shape. Look out in agricultural supply shops for very cheap offers of ex-fertiliser buckets. They need to be well-scrubbed.

4 Flags and canes Any gardening shop will sell you garden canes made of bamboo. You will need the ones measuring 4 feet (1.2 m) in length. For litter-carrying canes, simply bind each end with insulating tape to prevent splitting.

Use scrap material and remnants to make the flags. Cut them in triangles, allowing an extra 2 inches (5 cm) at the staff end, to form a wide hem. Stitch across the top. The finished flag is slipped over the end of the cane and secured with insulating tape.

5 Bins The most appropriate size is the swing-lid bin, minus its top. It can be used inverted when a table is required. Alternatively, make a special table top out of softwood which will fit into the open end of the bin. This is necessary, for example, in the Pyramid Race, where the base of the bin would be too small to hold four ice-cream boxes. (See drawings.)

6 Old socks Just the answer for anyone wondering what to do with odd socks: save them up and hand them over to your local games squad. Most games using old socks (Old Sock Race, Aunt Sally) require them rolled up into a ball. A single sock treated this way is not substantial enough, so you can screw up a sheet of newspaper and stuff it into the toe of the sock before rolling it up. Stitch along the end to prevent the sock from coming undone. If possible, use brightly coloured socks which can easily be seen.

7 Mugs Two types of mugs are used in gymkhana games. Prince Philip Cup competitions favour metal mugs with handles, which can be bought at camping shops. They do not stack, however, so for a race which requires three or more mugs on top of a pole you will need plastic beakers (available at hardware shops). Plastic throwaway cups can also be used. They are cheap to buy in quantity or can be saved from giant packets of washing powder, but they are not very durable and an organiser would need plenty of spares.

8 Balls Tennis balls are most commonly used, as rubber balls are too bouncy, and foam plastic ones are too light. Buy the cheapest you can find. For a race such as Ball and Racquet – where it may be necessary for a rider to locate and pick up a dropped ball – it is a good idea to provide different coloured balls for each lane. In the shops, tennis balls tend to be white or yellow, but blue dye can be used on white balls to produce blue ones and on yellow balls to provide green ones. Red dye gives pink/red and orange respectively.

9 Bottles Save one-litre squash bottles similar in shape, and weight them with sand. If you want to paint them to make them readily visible, first cover them with fabric adhesive tape. The paint can make them brittle, and it is very unfortunate for riders and organiser alike if a bottle disintegrates during a race. They are less easy to squash if they are one-third filled with sand and topped up with plastic bean-bag beans.

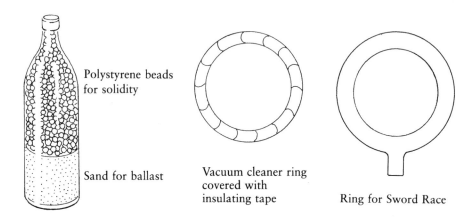

Polystyrene beads for solidity

Sand for ballast

Vacuum cleaner ring covered with insulating tape

Ring for Sword Race

10 Rings For the Ring Race, rubber vacuum cleaner rings are used in large quantities (no fewer than 54 for six lanes) and the initial outlay, therefore, is quite high. But they are very durable. They need to be bound in coloured insulating tape to make them readily visible: if possible using a different colour for each lane.

The other type of ring, used in the Sword Race, is made of metal or wood, shaped as shown in the drawing. The internal diameter is 4 inches (10 cm), the overall diameter 6 inches (15 cm), and it has a straight piece for fixing it to the post.

11 Litter When it was first introduced, the Litter Race called for all types of empty cartons, but the rules of the game now confine themselves to one-litre plastic washing-up liquid containers, cut off at the shoulder. To provide enough of these for six lanes, a concerted effort is required by the organiser and helpers. It takes quite a long time to finish a bottle, and all concerned must be warned not to throw empty ones away. They are fairly robust and can usually be pushed back into shape even after being trodden on. Spares should always be at hand.

12 Extra equipment Under this heading can be grouped all the miscellaneous items needed for special races. Once acquired, these can be used again and again. If you are a regular organiser of gymkhanas you quickly develop a squirrel instinct: never turning down anything which might come in useful. Old shirts, old shoes, sacks of all kinds (hessian ones are becoming harder to find), lengths of rope, motor cycle tyres – the list of handy objects gets longer and longer. Some items have to be made specially for a particular race –

wooden swords, for example, and old tennis racquets to which crosspieces have been added – but once made or bought they last for years.

Storage   If possible, try to store all equipment in one place. A small garden shed is ideal. Before the season begins, you can go through the items, checking that everything is there and repairing or replacing where necessary. A small trailer with a hinged lid is best for transporting equipment, and will save time when you are setting up or dismantling an arena.

7
Saddlery and Dress

Rules for saddlery and dress are constantly evolving, so this chapter can be no more than a general guide. Anyone taking part in team games should be familiar with the latest rules for the Pony Club Prince Philip Cup competition. For other shows and gymkhanas, read the schedule or, if in doubt, telephone the organiser.

If the organiser is heavily involved with the Pony Club, the rules are likely to conform to current Pony Club thinking. Otherwise, you may find that standards of dress are fairly casual, and that no rules at all are laid down for bitting and saddlery.

The only rules nowadays which seem to be universal are a total ban on the use of whips and spurs and an insistence on the wearing of hard hats. At Pony Club events, hats must conform to the following standards: PAS015, EN1384 (both with either BSI Kitemark or SEI) or ASTM F1163 (with SEI). Hats must be worn with the chin strap correctly fastened at all times when mounted; this includes prize-giving when mounted. Hat covers must be dark blue or black. The No. 5 rider, when taking part unmounted, must also wear a hat (fastened).

When organising a gymkhana open to all, it is wise to state clearly on the schedule exactly what is and is not allowed. For example, on a hot day are riders permitted to wear T-shirts or to ride with shirt sleeves rolled up? If you do not make it perfectly clear, you may well find a rider turning up in a bikini top! At the same time, very formal riding wear is not necessary at gymkhanas. Given the athletic nature of many gymkhana games, sweatshirts and jerseys are more sensible than tweed jackets. Showing jackets should definitely be discouraged.

□ It seems reasonable to insist on jodhpurs or breeches rather than jeans. For safety's sake, trainers and wellington boots should be banned. In the absence of jodhpur boots or riding boots, shoes with a smooth sole and well-defined heel should be worn.

□ In the Prince Philip Cup competition, riders must wear long-sleeved white shirts with Pony Club ties. On cold days, white V-neck sweaters may be worn over shirts, and in wet weather colourless or white waterproof cagoules with long sleeves are permitted. Tabards in team colours are worn on top. Hat covers must be dark blue or black.

Ponies don't all have to match, but they must be well turned out, their tack clean and in good repair. Riding clothes and footwear should be spotless.

Everything will be thoroughly examined at the tack inspection – and once passed cannot be changed.

☐ Whichever type of saddlery you use, it must be sound and well-fitting. Prince Philip Cup rules stipulate leather saddles with a conventional hunting/general purpose tree, and girths with two buckles. Martingales may be used – but only standing, running, Irish or bib martingales, worn and fitted correctly. Running martingales may not be adapted for use as a standing martingale. Standing martingales may not be attached to a drop noseband. A grakle or flash noseband is acceptable in place of a plain drop, but the Kineton noseband is forbidden.

☐ The bit allowed in the Prince Philip Cup is a plain snaffle with a smooth mouthpiece, which may be jointed or straight. Bitless bridles, including hackamores, are not permitted.

☐ In the Prince Philip competition there is always a tack inspection before the games, when every item of saddlery can be, and usually is, minutely inspected – not simply for cleanliness but also for soundness and safety. Woe betide any rider whose leathers show frayed stitching! Saddles must not be down on the withers. Leather straps must not show cracks or splits. Any item which fails the test may be changed, as long as the replacement passes the approval of the Official Steward. When the inspection has been completed, no rider may substitute any piece of equipment.

☐ In a gymkhana open to anybody, however, it is not possible without prior warning to carry out an inspection of all who are taking part. The organiser may lay down certain rules in the schedule, and contravention of these rules can lead to the disqualification of the rider concerned. But it is rare for a gymkhana schedule to state, for example, that Pelham bits or hackamores may not be worn. And should you – in a leading-rein class, say – turn away a Shetland pony because he is wearing a simple pad saddle without a tree? The discretion of the organiser in these instances needs to be fairly generous. Some ponies go better in Pelham bits than plain snaffles. If the bit fits the pony and if the chain is not twisted or too tight, there is no need to turn the competitor away.

At all times, judges and organisers alike should look out for serious faults. Some may arise through ignorance and can be corrected straightaway by tactful suggestion. A bit that is too low or too high in the pony's mouth, a twisted curb chain, or a badly adjusted crupper or martingale, can be discreetly corrected. Rough riding, on the other hand, must be stopped immediately, especially if coupled with poor tack.

Organisers are in a position to give advice to those whose main fault is lack of knowledge. If, in the process, they can steer children towards membership of the Pony Club, so much the better.

'A quick word of advice'.

8
Judging and Line Stewarding

At ordinary gymkhanas, judging means a great deal more than simply deciding which rider crosses the line first. If you are invited to judge the gymkhana events at a show, you will almost invariably set up the equipment, act as collecting-ring steward and as starter, settle arguments, take late entries, and clear up afterwards. Sometimes, you will also be expected to provide the equipment and to write the rules.

Be prepared, therefore, to *earn* your title of judge. Do not, for example, expect to start at the time stated on the schedule. Inevitably there will either be a class already taking place in the ring designated for gymkhana events, or half the competitors will be in other rings competing in minimus jumping or best rider or family pony. Inevitably, too, the rain which has been forecast, will hold off until the very moment that you start your duties. Gymkhana judges need good waterproofs and plenty of stamina.

It helps if organiser and judge can meet beforehand to discuss the events and to settle rules. If, as a gymkhana judge of long standing, you already possess equipment, you may wish to provide it yourself, together with an assistant. Sometimes, you will be offered an assistant: in any case, you can never have too many.

Although the actual classes are listed in the schedule, many shows stipulate entries on the day of competition. Some show organisers issue tickets to the competitors which are handed to the judge or steward at the ringside: the idea being to prevent unauthorised entrants, who may not have paid entry fees, from taking part. These tickets – usually raffle tickets – are just a nuisance. The judge quickly acquires a pocketful of scrappy bits of paper, and just as quickly forgets who has handed in tickets and who has not. A much easier method of checking entries is for the judge to be given a complete list of entrants as soon as the class has closed. She can then take a roll call of the children waiting in the collecting ring, tick them off on her list, call for those who are missing (a loud hailer is a useful asset) and collect entry fees from any extras.

She can also rapidly work out the number of heats required and the number needed to be kept from each heat to finish with six for the final.

Usually it is not too difficult to pick out the first, second and, if necessary, the third in each heat. Difficulty arises when there is a close contest for the places. It is impossible for one person to put six riders into the correct order and to remember which one is which – one grey pony looks very like another in the heat of the moment. It is essential to have assistance, preferably five helpers, so that each of you can watch for a specific position and remember which child occupied it. There are usually enough parents or other adults around the ring who will willingly help if required.

It is easier to judge the result of a Prince Philip competition because the riders wear identifying colours. However, if possible, judges should be provided with a raised dais or flat trailer placed on the finishing line, thus enabling them to view the finish from above. At ground level, the optical effect makes the rider furthest from the judge appear to be ahead even though she may, in fact, be anything up to half a length behind.

At ordinary gymkhanas, mistakes by judges are rarely questioned. Usually they occur when a rider has failed to carry out the rules of the race correctly and the error has been overlooked by the judge. In a Ride and Run race, for example, stirrups have not been crossed, or in a Bending race a pole has been missed. Often, spectators will point out the error, and it is then up to the judge to decide what remedy to take. In any dispute the simplest solution is either to disqualify the offending competitor or to call for a straight run-off between the particular riders.

Objections on grounds other than the actual running of the race may well be addressed to the judge, but these should immediately be referred to the organiser. It is not the judge's job to decide whether a rider is too old for a class or if a pony is too big. A common complaint is against a child in a leading-rein class who has been seen riding off the leading-rein elsewhere in the show. Organisers should always make certain that the rules are clearly stated in the schedule.

Line stewarding

The line steward is an important member of the Prince Philip Cup squad. In all inter-branch contests, including friendly competitions, each team taking part is expected to provide one line steward, or maybe two if not enough teams have entered to produce the minimum of twelve stewards required for a team competition.

Each of the six lanes in the contest is monitored during play by two line stewards, one at each end. Armed with number boards corresponding to the number of the lane which they are stewarding, they watch a team closely as it takes part. If an error occurs, the steward spotting the mistake raises the number board. This is repeated by the corresponding steward at the other end of the arena. As soon as the mistake has been corrected, the boards are lowered. The point of raising boards at both ends is to enable riders to realise, without turning round, that a fault has occurred and that it must be put right before their team can continue the race. A raised board is also the means of informing the Official Steward that something is amiss. If one team obstructs another, the line steward of the offending team should not raise the board until the heat has been completed. It is then up to the Official Steward to decide what penalty should be incurred.

To be a good line steward, it is necessary to concentrate on the job in hand and to be alert. Most line stewards start off in this way, but as the competition progresses, their attention begins to waver. They may, for example, forget to raise the number board in response to the action of their partner at the other end – or, having raised it, to put it down again. By tradition, line stewards do not judge the lane in which their own team is performing, changing places instead with the line steward next door. But their team is still in the arena and it takes a real effort of will not to have one eye on them instead of devoting your whole attention to your own lane.

Line stewards must be familiar with the rules of the games. Surprisingly, this is not always the case, particularly in minor competitions. The best way in which to familiarise yourself totally with a game and the problems or errors which can occur, is to attend the practices regularly. If any queries arise during practice, the time to find an answer to them is during the briefing which always precedes a competition and which is, or should be, attended by all line stewards and team trainers. The Chief Steward or Official Steward, who conducts the briefing, can then make a ruling. It may be a snap judgement but, as long as it is made with authority, it will apply for that particular competition. It is up to the team trainer to carry the information back to her team.

One of the best ways of training line stewards is for an Area to conduct its own study day, inviting all branches within the Area who have mounted games teams to send representatives. The programme could consist, first, of a demonstration by two invited teams of the games selected for the current year, with discussion and questions after each game. Then, would-be line stewards should take part in a practical demonstration, with each of the two teams deliberately making errors: the children themselves deciding which errors to make and when. The children enjoy doing this and can be quite ingenious in dreaming up 'mistakes'. Finally, there can be an overall discussion, allowing problems to be aired and solutions put forward.

If possible, such a study day should be held in an indoor school, with a viewing gallery to accommodate the visitors. Refreshments will be needed and a small charge to cover the costs can be made to branches taking part.

The result of such a study day would be an immediate rise in the standard of line stewarding.

9
Rally Games

In the Pony Club Year Book, under the guidelines for Working Rallies, it is recommended that the working rally day should be divided into periods and that some time should be devoted to mounted games. This does not always happen: although most branches include fun rallies in their programmes. But whether the rule book is followed faithfully or whether the 'fun' part is a separate event, it can be quite a headache for rally organisers to think up ideas. The following suggestions might help. Some are particularly suited to camp activities, where the children are already divided into groups according to the ability of both pony and rider.

Balloon Bursting

Two teams of five. Each member of the team has a balloon attached to the middle of her back. The aim is to burst the balloons of the opposing team in one or two minutes. A rider whose balloon has burst must retire from the game. When time is up, the team with the greatest number of survivors is the winner.

It is best if this can be played in a clearly defined area (to prevent riders from disappearing over the horizon). A whistle or siren should signal the start and finish. Preparation (blowing up balloons) is lengthy but the game is enjoyable. With several teams, a knockout contest could be held.

Changing Ponies

Divide the riders into two teams and line them up facing a cone or similar marker. Each rider should have an unmounted partner. On the signal to start (a whistle or the drop of a flag), the first pair of both teams ride and run to their marker where they change places and return together to the end of their line. The next pair then set off. When all the pairs have completed their runs, all the riders in the team dismount and stand at their ponies' heads. The first team to reach this stage is the winner.

Cowboys and Indians

This is a game best played in woodland where there are plenty of well-defined paths and rides. Riders separate into two teams, Cowboys and Indians, with one team – the Indians, say – being issued with hatbands, sashes or some other means of identification. Each rider is given a raffle or cloakroom ticket – red for Indians and blue or white for Cowboys.

Select a suitable clearing as a Checkpoint and send the teams into the wood with a five-minute interval between the two teams. The riders should spread out, and may hide and ambush their opponents if they wish. When a Cowboy spots an Indian, or vice versa, he challenges him, calling out: 'Halt!' Both riders then produce their tickets and the one with the lower number must surrender it to the other before returning to the Checkpoint to collect another ticket.

At the end of an allotted time, a whistle is sounded or a hooter or horn is blown, and all riders immediately gather at the Checkpoint. The team which has collected the greatest number of opponents' tickets is the winner.

If there are many young riders or beginners present, members of each team may work in pairs, one ticket only being issued to each pair.

Cushion Polo

This game is not suitable for beginners but is excellent for competent riders, particularly at Pony Club camp where it should be possible to organise a tournament.

Equipment Cushion made from a sheet of foam plastic, 18 inches (46 cm) square, sewn into canvas to form a sausage • Chestnut stake, 4 feet (1.2 m) high, with a small platform, 18 inches (46 cm) by six inches (15 cm), mounted on its top • Flags to mark the corners of the ground and the goal posts • Coloured tabards or sashes to distinguish the teams • Whistle for the umpire.

Ground The game is played on a flat pitch measuring between 80 and 120 yards or metres long by 30 to 50 yards or metres wide. There is a goal, marked by flags 4 yards or metres apart, at each end. The stake with the platform on top is mounted in the centre of the ground.

Teams Teams consist of four players.

Time allowed The game is played in chukkas of five minutes' duration. No allowance is made for stoppages. There will usually be a three-minute interval between chukkas, but if several teams are playing, it is possible to alternate the chukkas, allowing the ponies a longer period of rest. The number of chukkas per match is decided beforehand, but three chukkas are usually sufficient to produce a result.

Rules

1 At the start of the game, the cushion is placed on the centre platform. Each member of the team stands to the north, east, south and west of the centre stake alongside a member of the opposing team.

2 When the umpire blows his whistle, the north pair ride for the platform. The first of the two riders to reach it takes the cushion and places it under her left upper arm.

3 The cushion must be passed to each member of the team in turn, either from hand to hand or by being thrown and caught.

4 Only when every player in the team has had possession of the cushion – that is, has held it correctly tucked under her arm, not merely touched it – can a goal be scored.

5 A goal is scored when the fourth team member carries the cushion, correctly held, between the goal posts. The cushion cannot be thrown through or carried through in the hand.

6 When a goal has been scored, or at the start of a new chukka, the cushion is replaced on the central platform and the next pair, moving clockwise around the compass, ride in to grab the cushion.

7 A team loses possession of the cushion if it is snatched by one of the opposing players or if a pass is intercepted. The snatch may only be made from the near side – that is, the side on which the player is carrying the cushion. A player may not lean across an opponent's pony to grab the cushion.

8 Immediately a player gains the cushion, either by a snatch or an intervention, it must be put under his or her left arm. Failure to release the cushion constitutes a foul, punishable by having possession awarded to the challenger.

9 The cushion can be held in the hand only if it is intercepted or snatched when it is being passed to a fellow team member.

10 If the cushion is dropped, or if a foul is committed, the umpire will blow his whistle. Play is then stopped while the cushion is handed to the umpire, who will pass it to a member of the team which neither dropped the cushion nor caused the foul. All other players retire 5 yards or metres.

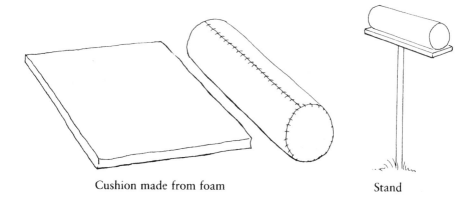

Cushion made from foam   Stand

11 The cushion is out of play if it is carried over the baseline but not through the goal pasts. The game is stopped, and the umpire carries the cushion into the field of play 5 yards or metres from the point where the baseline was crossed. He gives it to a member of the team which did not take it out of play, while the remaining players retire 5 yards or metres.

12 If the cushion is carried over the sideline, the umpire must use his discretion as to whether it has gone out of play. A deliberate crossing of the sideline to avoid an opponent would constitute a foul, but a minor infringement would not be penalised. In the case of a foul, the umpire should take action in the same way as when the baseline is crossed.

13 Riding off is allowed. A player may ride off an opponent who is not in possession of the cushion if that player is attempting to receive or intercept a pass. Crossing, pushing the elbows or hands, or kicking or beating an opponent's pony are all fouls.

14 Teams change ends after a goal has been scored or at the start of a new chukka.

Umpire It is very important for the umpire to be firm, fair and respected. He must, of course, be mounted. In a tournament, it is better to have two mounted umpires, each controlling one half of the field of play. It may also help to have linesmen. The umpire or umpires must be prompt and strict about dealing with rough or dangerous play. If necessary, players persistently committing fouls should be sent off, either for the remainder of the chukka or for the rest of the game.

Tactics With practice, riders can become very skilled at cushion polo, and when played well it is a fast and exciting game. If you are introducing it to riders who have never played before, it is best at first to bring in a trotting-only rule while the players are learning the principles of passing and interception. They will then know how to position themselves correctly so that passes can be made with the minimum amount of fuss, and to mark their opponents fairly and safely. Riders are not allowed to wear spurs nor to carry whips.

Follow-My-Leader

This can be fun for all riders, whatever standards they have reached, as long as the leader is experienced, sensible and enterprising. If possible, this game should take place over natural terrain, where there are small ditches and bushes to jump. A rider must keep one pony's length from the rider in front.

Fox and Hound

Riders are divided into pairs. They then form a large circle, facing outwards, with the two riders in each pair standing one behind the other. One pair is chosen to be the fox and hound. The hound chases the fox around the outside of the circle and attempts to catch the fox by touching that rider's sleeve. At any time the fox may 'go to earth' by riding into the circle and standing behind one of the waiting pairs. The front rider of the pair then becomes the hound and the previous hound the fox. If a hound catches a fox, the roles are reversed. The game continues indefinitely.

Grandmother's Footsteps

This is an ideal game for beginners, but is best when played in a confined space such as an indoor or outdoor manège. The riders line up at one end while the organiser or instructor stands at the other, with her back to the riders. The riders attempt to creep up on 'grandmother' without her noticing them. From time to time she turns round, hoping to spot one or more of the riders moving forward. If she sees them she calls out their names and they must return to the baseline and start again. The winner is the first to reach the 'grandmother' undetected.

Handkerchief Snatching

Players separate into teams of four, each rider carrying a handkerchief tucked under her left arm, which she is not allowed to touch with her hand. The players try to snatch the handkerchiefs away from the members of the opposing team *within two minutes*. Once a player loses her handkerchief, she drops out of the game. If she lets her handkerchief fall, she may dismount to retrieve it. Only at this point is she allowed to touch her own handkerchief with her hand. An opponent may also try to retrieve the dropped handkerchief by dismounting, but if in the process she also drops her handkerchief, both players remount and continue the game.

He

(see Touch)

Horseman's Post

This game needs some preparation, but once the initial work has been done, the equipment can be used again and again.

Equipment   Several cardboard boxes (i.e. the posting boxes) with slits cut in their lids • Several sets of coloured cards bearing the names of, say, famous show jumpers or racehorses, or parts of the saddle and bridle and of the horse. Each set should have the same names. The choice is up to the organiser but the boxes must carry the same names as the cards. The boxes are distributed around the fields or woods where the game is to be played.

Instructions Riders are divided into pairs, and a set of coloured cards is assigned to each pair. The cards are kept at a central point (the Post Office). A card of the appropriate colour is handed to each pair. They then have to post it in the correct posting box. Before they are handed out the sets of cards should be shuffled so that the pairs are all looking for different boxes. As soon as a card has been correctly posted, the pair return to the Post Office to receive another one.

The game can be made more difficult by making the names on the cards and boxes different, though linked – for example, a famous rider on the card (e.g. Mark Todd) and his horse on the box (Charisma), or grakle on the card and noseband on the box.

Hunt the Ribbons

A good game for beginners but one which requires preparation. Each rider is given a piece of coloured ribbon: a different colour for each child. More pieces of ribbon are hidden round the field or wood, six of each colour, and the riders have to search for them. The first to return with a complete set of seven pieces is the winner. If there are more riders than colours, the game may be played in pairs.

Mime Game

Divide the riders as evenly as possible into teams. At a signal to start, the first rider from each team comes out to the organiser or steward and is given an action to perform in front of the other members of the team. The actions should be connected with horses: for example, filling a haynet, putting on a saddle, cleaning a bridle, mucking out, etc. When the action has been identified correctly, the next rider canters to the organiser and receives the next instruction. When all the members of the team have carried out their mimes successfully, the captain informs the organiser. The first team to complete all their mimes is the winner.

Mock Hunt

The Mock Hunt is a first-class introduction to hunting manners and practice, and is worthy of a rally all to itself. However, it requires a great deal of planning as well as the co-operation of local farmers and landowners, and it involves more work than one person could manage on her own.

Three experienced riders should be chosen to play the principal roles – those of the Fox, the Huntsman and the Field Master. Reliable associates can usually fulfil these parts extremely well. A day or two before the Mock Hunt is due to take place, the three principals should meet together and plan the course of the hunt – the country over which the hunt will take place, the movements of the fox, the coverts to be drawn by the hounds, where the fox will break, etc, and where the field will assemble to watch hounds at work.

Capable members should be chosen to act as whippers-in and hounds. Two whippers-in, and no more than two couple of hounds, should be sufficient. All these riders must be readily identifiable. The fox could wear a yellow jersey or tabard, the hounds brown or brown and white, the huntsman and whips red jerseys. The Field Master can wear a black coat.

The hounds must be taught to give tongue and to cast. They must be told to obey the Huntsman at all times. If possible, the Huntsman should be able to blow simple calls on his horn.

The fox must be provided with a bag of woodshavings or sawdust, with which to lay a trail. The Huntsman will of course know the line that the fox intends to take, but the hounds will not, and the Huntsman must take care not to put hounds on to the line too quickly for fear that the fox will be caught and 'killed' before the field have had a chance to see hounds in action and to enjoy a run.

The fate of the fox should be decided beforehand, either a 'kill' or 'gone to ground'. If it is to be a 'kill', all the traditions can be followed: a mock 'brush' made of unravelled rope may be presented to a deserving follower, biscuits can substitute for breaking up the fox, and tomato ketchup can be used to 'blood' members.

A Mock Hunt offers an ideal opportunity to explain what hunting is all about. Before it begins, the Master can outline what is going to happen and can explain the role of the followers. Afterwards, before 'Home' is blown, he can give advice on hacking or boxing home and what to do on arrival.

As a means of combining useful lessons on the art of hunting and behaviour in the hunting field, which will stand members in good stead in the future, with an excellent ride across country, the Mock Hunt is hard to beat.

Paper Chase

An advanced form of follow-my-leader, the paper chase is one of the oldest recreations in the Pony Club. If possible, it should be held over a wide and varied terrain with plenty of natural jumps such as ditches and small bushes. Sawdust or woodshavings, rather than paper, should be used to lay the trail, unless someone is prepared to go round afterwards and clear up the litter. Two riders are chosen to lay the chase, including plenty of false trails, and they set off about half-an-hour before the rest of the field.

Quiz Game

Divide the riders into teams, roughly comparable in ability: for example, a team could consist of two holders of D Test, two of C, one of C+ and one of B. Each team is allotted a steward, who stands in front of the riders, armed with a list of questions and answers. The first member of the team comes forward and is given a question. As soon as she has answered it correctly, she returns to her team and another rider takes her place. If she cannot answer the question, she sends the next member of her team to answer it. The winner is the team which completes its question-paper first.

Round the World

Not to be confused with the exercise of the same name. In this instance, the riders are divided into two teams and numbered in each team from 1 upwards. All riders then form a large circle, facing inwards, the teams intermingling so that the order is haphazard. The instructor picks a number at random – 5, for example – and calls out: 'Number 5, at the canter (or walk or trot): *go!*' Both riders bearing number 5 leave the circle and proceed right round the outside at the prescribed pace until they reach their place again. The first to return gains a point for her team.

Scavenger Hunt

There are various ways of tackling this ever-popular rally game, but all of them require the provision of plastic sandwich bags and sometimes the preparing of a list. The simplest form is to give each participant a bag and to send them out with the instruction to bring back as many objects beginning with a particular letter as they can. It is important to set a time limit – an hour is about right. At the end, you count up the collections, and the one with the most objects is the winner. If you have a mixture of novice and more competent riders, it is best to separate them into pairs so that there is always one to hold both ponies while the other dismounts to retrieve an object.

Another version is to make a list of some 15 items which have to be collected. Before making the list, you must be familiar with the area in which the riders will be searching, so that you do not ask for something which cannot be found. Include items such as a horseshoe-nail or a leather strap and see how many of them realise that these come with the pony! Always tell the riders a time when they must be back, in order to avoid the lengthy and tiresome business of rounding up stragglers.

The lists can be as long or as short as you wish: a number of varied objects, or a list of items on a linked theme, such as wild flowers (choose the common varieties) or leaves from different trees.

If you think that the competitors will complete their collections too quickly, finish up with an anagram of, say, a well-known horse or rider (e.g. NI YGN GNLE).

Simon Says

A good game for young riders, although any age can take part. Riders stand or circle round an instructor who calls out orders, such as: 'Feet out of stirrups!' or 'Dismount!' The orders must be obeyed but only when prefaced by the words: 'Simon says'. If anyone makes a mistake, she either drops out or loses a point.

Smugglers and Excisemen

This is a good team game to be played on common land or in woods where there is plenty of cover and plenty of room. The equipment will need to be prepared beforehand, but once collected or made it can be used again.

Equipment About three dozen brightly-coloured cotton reels (painted red or orange) • Three small plastic bins • Several lengths of thin cord about 12 feet (3.7 m) long • One flag, bearing a skull and crossbones • Two signs, one with the name of an inn, the other with the words CUSTOMS HOUSE on it • Coloured hat-covers or sashes to distinguish the excisemen from the rest.

Instructions Decide where to position the Customs House, the Inn and the Smugglers' Ship, and set up the appropriate signs. The ship and inn should be about half to one mile apart, the Customs House perhaps midway between, so that the three bases form a triangle. Place a bin at each point and fill the one at the ship sign with the cotton reels. Divide the children into pairs and issue about one-third of them with hat covers or sashes. These are the Excisemen. Give each of the remaining pairs – the Smugglers – a length of cord, and send the Smugglers to their ship and the Excisemen to the Customs House.

The object of the game is for the Smugglers to carry as many kegs of brandy (cotton reels) as they can from the ship to the Inn without being stopped by Excisemen. The Smugglers must transfer only one keg at a time. They carry it by threading a cotton reel on to their piece of cord, with each member of the pair holding an end of the cord. The Excisemen try to make the Smugglers drop their keg. If this happens – which it will do if one of the pair lets go of her end of the cord – the Smugglers immediately return to their ship for another keg. The Excisemen retrieve the fallen keg and carry it away to the Customs House, where they deposit it in the bin. While they are in charge of a keg, they cannot chase any other Smugglers they may see.

The game is started by a blast on a whistle and continues for a predetermined time. Another whistle-blast is the signal for all players to go to their respective bases: the Smugglers to the Inn, the Excisemen to the Customs House. There the kegs in the two bins are counted, and the side with the greatest number wins.

Touch

This is best played in a confined area. Any number of riders can take part. One rider starts as 'He' and the others scatter while the first rider tries to catch someone by touching her on the arm. The rider who has been touched then becomes 'He' and the game continues.

Touch Wood

A similar game to Touch, but it must be played in a field where there are several trees, wooden fence posts, gates, etc. The catcher attempts to catch anyone who is not touching wood. To be caught successfully, the quarry must be touched on the left arm. To keep the game going, the instructor or steward should have a whistle and use it to signal that every rider must move from one piece of wood to another. The catcher's role passes each time a rider is touched.

Treasure Hunt

A treasure hunt must be organised by someone who has an intimate knowledge of the terrain and the time to prepare the clues. The object of the game is to find hidden treasure by following a series of clues, each clue leading to the next. The clues can be in various forms:

☐ Anagrams. Solve an anagram and the answer shows where the next anagram can be found.
☐ Rhyming couplets.
☐ A series of questions: the answer to each being a number. Put the numbers together and the solution is a grid reference. It might be necessary in this instance to issue the competitors with ordnance survey maps.
☐ A fairly simple description of where clues and treasure are hidden.
☐ Collecting letters previously fixed to trees or fences or chalked on stones or rocks. Assemble the letters to find the name of a well-known show jumper, eventer or jockey.

If younger riders are taking part, it is often best to pair them with older riders. To avoid the problem of one pair following another round the course, issue each pair with a different set of clues, or start them from different places.

True and False

This is another game which requires a certain amount of careful preparation. First, inscribe a number of postcards with statements, which may be true or false. Each card should be numbered. Then pin or tie the cards to trees, fence posts, etc, within a given area. Divide the riders into pairs, and give each pair a sheet of paper and a pencil. Their objective is to find as many of the cards as they can, and to write down whether the statement that each card bears is true or false.

When everyone has finished, or when the time limit is up, the answers are collected. The pair with the most correct answers are the winners.

Examples of possible statements are:

☐ Always water after feeding your pony.
☐ A surcingle is another name for a Knight Bachelor.
☐ A fox's tail is called a brush.
☐ 'All on' means no one has fallen off.
☐ The Derby is run at Aintree.

Waterloo

A number of flags are set up in cones or bins behind a baseline. Some 50 yards or metres away is another line of cones or bins. The riders are divided into two teams and one team is issued with identifying tabards or sashes.

At the start of the game, one team lines up in a row in front of the baseline, facing the other team who line up just behind the row of cones. When the whistle signals the start of the game, the attacking team on the centre line attempts to capture the flags behind the baseline and to carry them back to the empty cones in the centre. The defending team must prevent them from doing this. An attacker is caught if she is touched by a defender. She then becomes a prisoner and must stand behind the baseline. An attacker who successfully penetrates the defence may either pick up a flag or release a prisoner, who must return to the centre before rejoining the attack. As soon as she crosses the baseline into the field of play she is vulnerable to recapture.

After an agreed period of time, a whistle is blown and the two teams exchange roles. The number of captured flags (that is, those in cones or bins on the centre line) are counted and the score is recorded. It is now the second team's turn to attempt to capture flags. At the end of the game, the team with the highest number of captured flags is the winner.

Both teams should be encouraged to plan their tactics. If wished, the defending team can have one flag which is bigger than the rest and which can only be captured by being carried between two attackers back to the centre line. It should, however, be worth more than the other flags.

10
Polocrosse

This game was developed in Australia just before World War 2, and since then has been widely played there and in Zimbabwe. In recent years it has become popular in many countries and was re-introduced to Britain in 1988. A mixture of polo and lacrosse, it is a fast and exciting game: probably best introduced at camp, or at a rally where an hour or two can be spared for enough members to be taught the general rules and then to play some chukkas. It is ideal for Pony Club members who are too old for mounted games.

Played well it requires great dexterity, but the basic skills are easily learned. As members are usually able to enjoy playing it after a very short time, there is unlimited incentive for them to improve their proficiency and the training of their ponies. Nearly all ponies and horses are suitable, as long as they do not kick or show vice. However, for a high standard game, a well-schooled pony is essential.

Equipment Each player needs a stick approximately 40 inches (1 m) to 42 inches long, with a loose net attached to an oval head. The ball is made of very soft, lightweight foam rubber, approximately 4 inches (10 cm) in diameter. A Branch starting to play should have a minimum of 6 sticks, and 2 balls.

Four goal posts, each 10 ft (3 m) high, are required. For complete beginners, shorter posts can be used. The posts must *give* if ridden into, and must not be fixed rigid.

The Field The field is 160 yds (146 m) long by 60 yds (55 m) wide, but a smaller field – say 120 yds (110 m) by 50 yds (45 m) – can be used for practice; for complete beginners the smaller field is probably best. If the field is not full-size, keep the penalty lines at 30 yards (27 m) and the semi-circles 11 yds (10 m) in radius, but reduce the size of the centre section. Goal posts should be 8 feet (2.4 m) apart.

Teams In the Championships and in formal tournaments a full team consists of 6 players, divided into 2 sections of 3 players each. The two sections play alternate chukkas, and a match can be of 4, 6 or 8 chukkas. However, most tournaments are organised on a league basis with single-section matches of one chukka. Chukkas can be of 6 to 8 minutes long, and there is an interval of 2 minutes between chukkas.

Players should wear numbered team shirts or tabards: No. 1 for Attack,

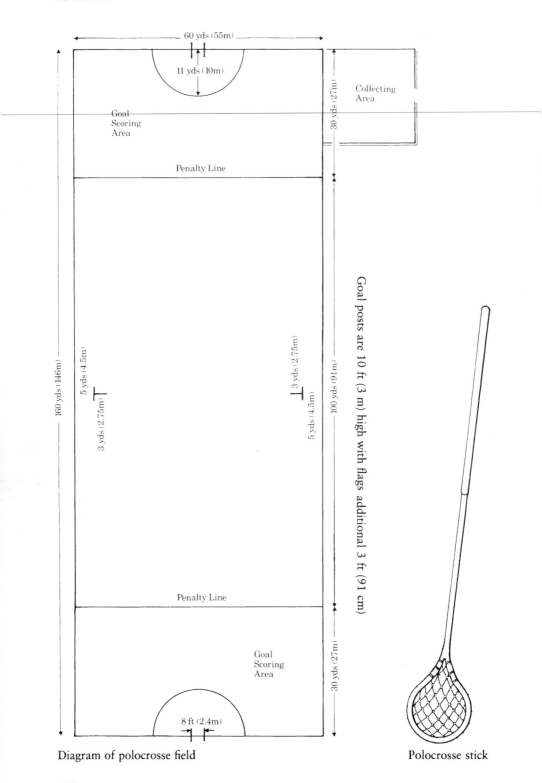

Diagram of polocrosse field

Polocrosse stick

No. 2 for Centre, and No. 3 for Defence. No. 1 may not play in the opposite team's goal-scoring area. No. 3 may not play in his own team's goal-scoring area. No. 2 plays only in the central section. Thus the attacking No. 1 and the defending No. 3 are the only players allowed in the relevant goal-scoring area.

Objects of the Game   To score more goals than your opponents. A goal is scored when the No. 1 throws the ball with his stick across the goal line between the goal posts – from within the goal scoring area, but outside the semi-circle.

Umpires   It is best to have two mounted umpires, each controlling one half of the field. However, one umpire can control a game of beginners or novices who do not play too fast. In addition there should be two unmounted goal judges, one behind each goal, whose job it is to determine whether a shot at goal passes between the goal posts.

Ponies   A player is allowed only one pony in a tournament. The size of the pony is usually limited for junior matches but not for open.

The Start   The game begins in centre field. The players line up in pairs side by side and one behind the other. Each team stands closest to the goal that it is defending. The No. 1s are in front, then the No. 2s, with the No. 3s at the back. All are facing the umpire, at least 5 yards (approx 4.5 m) from him. The umpire throws the ball overarm from the sideline high between the players. The game recommences similarly after a goal is scored.

Whenever an attempt at goal fails, No. 3 throws the ball back into play from just behind the penalty line.

Play   Players pick up the ball from the ground or catch it in the net of the stick. The ball is carried or thrown from player to player until the No. 1 (Attack) is in possession of it in the goal-scoring area, so as to be able to throw at goal. A player may not carry the ball over the penalty line, but must bounce it on the ground so that he does not have possession of it while crossing the line. He may, however, throw the ball to another player across the line.

A player carrying the ball in his net must carry it on his stick side, i.e. right-handed players carry it on the off-side of the pony, left-handed players on the near-side. A player may not carry the ball across the pony, but he may pick it up or catch it on the non-stick side provided he brings the stick back to his stick side immediately. Hitting at an opponent's stick – either to dislodge the ball or to prevent him from gaining possession of it – is allowed in an upward direction only. Hitting down is not allowed, as the pony's legs might be hit.

'Riding-off' is allowed, but crossing, stopping over the ball, or elbowing, are not allowed. The wedging or sandwiching of one player between two players 'riding-off' simultaneously, is dangerous play and is not allowed.

The player riding closest to the line where the ball has travelled has right of way over any other player. A player coming in from an angle must give way to a player on the line, unless he is far enough away not to cause the player on the line to have to stop or swerve to avoid him. Crossing the line is a foul.

Rules   For the rules the current *Pony Club Polocrosse Rule Book* should be studied. It is a simplified version of the Rule Book of the UK Polocrosse Association, but for the Pony Club it includes certain restrictions on saddlery.

Members can play until they leave the Pony Club when they are 21. Many tournaments have classes for under 12 year-olds and under 15 year-olds as well as open classes, so that members play with others approximately their own age. A Pony Club pamphlet called *A Guide to Teaching Polocrosse* may be of help to less experienced instructors.

Study day.

Appendix 1
Health, Safety and Welfare

1 Organisers of any form of show or competition must comply with current Health and Safety Executive rulings and should ensure that they are in possession of the required documents. These include risk assessment, accident report and RIDDOR forms. (For Pony Club run events a copy of the latest Health and Safety document is available from the Pony Club Office).

2 A Risk Assessment should be completed for every event and the appropriate measures taken to minimise accidents.

3 Similarly, adequate medical cover must be provided and advice on these requirements sought from the appropriate body. It must be remembered that Ambulance and First Aid personnel must be booked well in advance and the arrangements confirmed by letter.

Appendix 2
Public Liability and Insurance

There are two forms of liability which apply to privately-run gymkhanas:

1 **Public liability** This is the organising committee's legal liability for bodily injury and/or damage to the property of third parties caused through the fault or negligence of themselves or their servants (helpers, officials, stewards) in connection with the gymkhana.

2 **Contractual liability** This is liability accepted by the committee under a contract or agreement. It applies, for example, where a gymkhana is being held in a public park, and it would cover the cost of making good any damage caused by the gymkhana, and/or indemnify the local council (as owners of the park) against any claim made on them for public liability.

The Pony Club's general insurance, incorporated into the British Horse Society's policy, provides public liability cover for events run by a Pony Club branch for its members. In some circumstances contractual liability is also covered. When all the competitors are not members of the Pony Club but the show itself is being run under the aegis of a Pony Club branch, cover is usually available under the Pony Club's policy.

Gymkhana organisers should always check these points with Pony Club headquarters while the organisation of a show is still in its early stages. In many cases it is necessary to furnish headquarters with relevant facts about the proposed show – date, venue, duration, and expected number of competitors. Headquarters can then clear the proposal with the insurance brokers.

Organisers of any show which is not covered under the Pony Club's general policy should take out their own public liability cover. A telephone call to any local insurance broker (look in the Yellow Pages for names and numbers) will give them the opportunity to compare costs and to take out insurance which fulfils the requirements of their particular event.

In addition, organisers are advised to publish in the schedule of their show a disclaimer, on the following lines:

'The Organising Committee does not accept any liability for any accident, damage, injury or illness to horses, owners, riders, spectators, ground or any other person or property whatsoever.'

Finally: objections. These fall into two categories. The first covers objections which arise in the heat of the moment – e.g. an irregular action on the part of one of the competitors, such as knocking over a cone or a ball bouncing out of the bucket, both of which could be missed by a judge busy separating riders in a tight finish. The second applies to infringements of the regulations – e.g., a child over the age limit, a pony over the size limit, a previous winner claiming to be a novice, and so on.

The first category is the responsibility of the judge on the field. Most competitors appreciate that mistakes can be made, and if it is not possible to correct or reverse a decision, a sympathetic smile and apology from the judge will quickly defuse a situation. If necessary, the aggrieved competitor can be offered free entry to the next class, or the race can be run again. The latter solution is not very satisfactory, as the re-run may adversely affect competitors not involved in the dispute.

The second category is the responsibility of the organiser or organising committee, the Chief Steward, or some other adjudicator, and it is usual to insist that objections under this heading should be made in writing, accompanied by a deposit of, say, £5 or £10, and within a predetermined time limit. The evidence is presented to the committee, who should hear representations from both sides before making their judgement. The deposit is returned if the objection is upheld.

It is sensible, therefore, to include in the schedule a paragraph on the following lines:

'An official objection may only be made on the grounds of ineligibility of pony or rider. It must be made in writing to the Secretary within half-an-hour of the relevant event and must be accompanied by a deposit of £10. Should the objection not be upheld, the deposit may be forfeited. The adjudicator's decision will be final, and there will be no appeal'.

In Prince Philip Cup competitions, the rules governing objections are clearly laid out in the Mounted Games rule book, issued annually. Anyone intending to take part in the championships should read them carefully.

Appendix 3
How to Calculate Heats

Working out heats is always a headache, but it helps if you have some idea of what to do before being faced by a milling crowd of riders in a collecting ring. Most gymkhanas award six rosettes and therefore need to have six riders in a final. If you have only seven entries, which means leaving just one competitor out of the ribbons, it is better to conjure up a seventh lane of equipment and an extra rosette than to force four riders to compete for three places in the final. For any number from 8 upwards, the following table will help, as it shows how to divide entrants up into heats and semi-finals to produce six for the final.

If you have more than 36 entries, you would be well advised to divide the class into two sections and to run them as separate classes, offering rosettes for each class.

No. of entries	No. of heats	No. in each heat	No. to keep back	No. in semi-final	Keep from 'semi'	No. in final
8	2	4	3	-	-	6
9	2	1 of 4 / 1 of 5	3	-	-	6
10	2	5	3	-	-	6
11	2	1 of 5 / 1 of 6	3	-	-	6
12	2	6	3	-	-	6
13	3	2 of 4 / 1 of 5	2	-	-	6
14	3	1 of 4 / 2 of 5	2	-	-	6
15	3	5	2	-	-	6
16	3	2 of 5 / 1 of 6	2	-	-	6

No. of entries	No. of heats	No. in each heat	No. to keep back	No. in semi-final	Keep from 'semi'	No. in final
17	3	1 of 5 2 of 6	2	-	-	6
18	3	6	2	-	-	6
19	4	3 of 5 1 of 4	3	2 of 6	3	6
20	4	5	3	2 of 6	3	6
21	4	3 of 5 1 of 6	3	2 of 6	3	6
22	4	2 of 5 2 of 6	3	2 of 6	3	6
23	4	1 of 5 3 of 6	3	2 of 6	3	6
24	4	6	3	2 of 6	3	6
25	5	5	2	2 of 5	3	6
26	5	4 of 5 1 of 6	2	2 of 5	3	6
27	5	3 of 5 2 of 6	2	2 of 5	3	6
28	5	2 of 5 3 of 6	2	2 of 5	3	6
29	5	1 of 5 4 of 6	2	2 of 5	3	6
30	6	5	1 or 2	- 2 of 5	- 3	6 6
31	6	5 of 5 1 of 6	1	-	-	6
32	6	4 of 5 2 of 6	1	-	-	6
33	6	3 of 5 3 of 6	1	-	-	6
34	6	2 of 5 4 of 6	1	-	-	6
35	6	1 of 5 5 of 6	1	-	-	6
36	6	6	1	-	-	6

Appendix 4
Useful Addresses

It is helpful for any organiser to know whom to ask for assistance during the initial planning stage of a gymkhana. The following is a list of useful addresses:

• For information on team games, in particular the Pony Club *Rule Book, Mounted Games Video and Booklet,* which demonstrate and explain the rules and skills required for all the Prince Philip games in current use, the latest rule book, and advice on insurance:
Pony Club Headquarters
NAC Stoneleigh Park, Kenilworth
Warwickshire CV8 2RW
Tel: 02476 698300
Fax: 02476 696836
email: enquiries@pony-club.org.uk

• For rosettes, competitors' numbers, entry and judges' books, officials' badges, etc.: look in the classified advertisements section of equestrian periodicals. There are a number of rosette manufacturers, all of whom supply other show necessities. By obtaining catalogues and price lists early in your gymkhana planning stages you will have plenty of time to compare prices and to send in your order. Most rosette makers need at least three weeks in which to complete an order, but the longer you can give them the better. When sending the order you should give the date of the show and a clear indication of the wording required on the rosettes, as well as the colour and number of rosettes.

The simplest versions offered by most manufacturers are single-tier rosettes with 1st, 2nd, etc., in the centre, and without the name of the show. These are very cheap. Block-printing of rosettes does not add a great deal to the cost, but you should only consider more elaborate additions – extra tiers of ribbon, longer tails, concertina pleats, etc. – if you are sure that the number of entries will justify the expense. Sponsors may sometimes underwrite the cost of rosettes, especially if their name or product can be printed on the tails.

The choice of colours for rosettes rests with the organisers, but the Pony Club specifies *blue* for 1st, *red* for 2nd, *green* for 3rd, *yellow* for 4th, *pink* for 5th and *mauve* for 6th. At Pony Club shows there may also be *gold* for 'placed', *white* for highly commended and *pale blue* for specials. These colours often puzzle non-Pony Club competitors, as the traditional colours at other shows are red for 1st, blue for 2nd, yellow for 3rd and green for 4th. Orange is often chosen for 5th and brown for 6th. Two-tone, two- and three-tier rosettes are always popular.

Rosette manufacturers are well geared to supply all the needs of show organisers. Usually your order will be acknowledged by a printed postcard, and the rosettes themselves will arrive a few days before the show. Other items, such as entry books and back numbers, will be sent in advance. Try to resist the temptation to keep telephoning the manufacturers in the run-up to the show because you are convinced that they have forgotten your order. The chances of that happening are very unlikely!

If you can afford to order more rosettes than you need for one show, you can save money. Most makers reduce their rates per item for bulk orders.

• For gymkhana equipment approved by the Pony Club (ask for catalogue and price list):
Signam Ltd
Harris Road
Warwick
CV3 5FY
Tel: 01926 417300
email: kwilson@signam.co.uk

• For team sweatshirts with Pony Club badge and name of branch and team, and for white acrylic V-necked sweaters for Prince Philip cup teams, as well as a range of other clothing:
Wainwright, Middle Street
Dawlish, Dorchester
Dorset DT2 7LX
Tel: 01258 837364/380
Fax: 01258 837400

• For the Pony Club *Polocrosse Rule Book*, the *Guide to Teaching Polocrosse* and the *Rule Book of the UK Polocrosse Association*, contact Pony Club HQ. For polo-crosse sticks and balls:
Jessica Shearing
1 Highfield Court
Brackley
Northants NN13 7AG
Tel: 01299 832844
email: equineweb.com

'Willingness covers such virtues as being easy to catch'.

Index

Figures in *italics* refer to illustrations